Additional Praise for *Real American*

"A thoroughly riveting poetic memoir of a mixed-race woman questioning her identity and place in American life and culture. Genuinely inspiring."
—*San Francisco Chronicle*

"A candid, deeply personal look at race relations within a family and a nation, and a story that will feel familiar to anyone who hungers for a sense of belonging."
—*Chicago Tribune*

"Lythcott-Haims never comes to a tidy conclusion about how to view race relations in America, because there isn't one. By allowing us to witness a woman coming to terms with herself, and finding nothing but pride and love there, she offers a blueprint for how others might try to do the same."
—*The New York Times Book Review*

"Breaks the silence on what it means to grow up mixed-race in America. Her spare but powerful prose has an emotional rawness that will profoundly resonate with all readers and help many feel a little less alone."
—**Heidi W. Durrow,** *New York Times* **bestselling author of** *The Girl Who Fell from the Sky*

"A cathartic and bold truth-telling."
—**Danzy Senna, bestselling author of** *Caucasia* **and** *New People*

"A powerful memoir of poetic prose."
—*The Baltimore Sun*

"[A] brilliant, unflinching portrayal of what it's been like . . . to grow up in a racially paralyzed America . . . [Lythcott-Haims has] managed to fit the whole messy, beautiful truth between two covers."
—*Forbes*

"A bold, impassioned memoir that . . . sheds fresh light on race and discrimination in American society."
—*Publishers Weekly*

"*Real American* is a courageous, achingly honest meditation on what it means to come to consciousness as a mixed-race child and adult in a nation where Black lives weren't meant to matter."
—**Michelle Alexander,** *New York Times* **bestselling author of** *The New Jim Crow: Mass Incarceration in the Age of Colorblindness*

"A compelling, incisive, and thoughtful examination of race, origin, and what it means to be called an American. Engaging, heartfelt, and beautifully written, Lythcott-Haims explores the American spectrum of identity with refreshing courage and compassion."

—**Bryan Stevenson,** *New York Times* **bestselling author of** *Just Mercy: A Story of Justice and Redemption*

"A powerful, honest book that should be required reading for everyone."

—**Anita Amirrezvani, author of** *The Blood of Flowers* **and** *Equal of the Sun*

"*Real American* is beautifully written, heartbreaking, and a real page-turner. . . . An essential read for anyone who wishes to understand the conversation about racial injustice."   —**Jean Kwok,** *New York Times* **bestselling author of** *Mambo in Chinatown* **and** *Girl in Translation*

"To write with such an open heart about race and Blackness takes great courage. To do so in prose that is at once elegant and raw takes great talent."   —**Ayelet Waldman, bestselling author of** *Bad Mother* **and** *A Really Good Day*

"*Real American* fuses autobiography with politics, showing how the sinister nature of racism (institutional and otherwise) scars even those who may pass as unaffected."   —*Shelf Awareness*

"In a text that resembles a memoir, a prose poem, and an album of verbal snapshots, a writer from a mixed racial background chronicles her journey—and battle—to understand her racial identity. . . . Many potent and painful reminders that we have a long, long way to go regarding race and identity."   —*Kirkus Reviews*

"A true achievement . . . so much more than a personal memoir . . . [Lythcott-Haims] channels the shrewdness of Eula Biss and the compassion of Ta-Nehisi Coates."   —**Lee Daniel Kravetz, internationally bestselling author of** *Strange Contagion* **and** *Supersurvivors*

"Powerful . . . a memoir that [illuminates] the psychic cost of racism to those who are cast as 'other.' The journey of self-healing and the empowerment . . . is a story of triumph from which all of us can learn."

—**Beverly Daniel Tatum, author of** *Why Are All the Black Kids Sitting Together in the Cafeteria?* **and** *Can We Talk about Race?*

"Stands for, and stands up for, Americans who are questioned, confronted, disregarded, and unnerved by our citizen country . . . *Real American* will

be one of those books that is passed from hand to hand, with passages marked where readers find strong words that speak truth."
—**A. J. Verdelle, author of** *The Good Negress*

"A memoir isn't worth the paper on which it is printed if it is not, first and foremost, brutally honest. Julie Lythcott-Haims's memoir, *Real American,* is not only worth the paper on which it is written, it is priceless. *Real American* is the humorous and heartbreaking story of the coming-of-age of an American woman born to a Black father and a white mother. Lythcott-Haims writes movingly and courageously of her struggle to figure out to which race she belongs. . . . It isn't easy being biracial in this country; *Real American* compellingly and honestly tells you why."
—**LaDoris Hazzard Cordell, retired California judge and former vice provost at Stanford University**

"A poignant, sensitive, and oftentimes painful personal account of growing up as a biracial person in color-conscious contemporary America. This gem of a book provides compelling stories about how race permeates the American psyche and how it so heavily weighs on people 'too white to be Black and too Black to be white.'"
—**Albert Camarillo, professor of American history and founding director of Stanford University's Center for Comparative Studies in Race and Ethnicity**

"No punches pulled. The tortuous path of being and becoming and insisting as we each have a right to be a real American."
—**Mary Frances Berry, the Geraldine R. Segal Professor of American Social Thought at the University of Pennsylvania and former chairperson of the United States Commission on Civil Rights**

"In this raw, accessible exploration of what it is to be truly American, author Julie Lythcott-Haims offers up her lifelong struggle with racial identity and internalized oppression. Her fascinating family—prominent Black American father and resilient white British mother, married in newly independent West Africa—provides a front row to history, while Julie's journey—like that of so many civil rights babies—reveals the limitations of privilege, from getting an Ivy League degree and professional career, to marrying white and American-dreaming in the suburbs. A fearless invitation to the important conversations Black and white America needs to be having."
—**Faith Adiele, author of** *Meeting Faith* **and** *The Nigerian-Nordic Girl's Guide to Lady Problems*

"Shows once again, plainly and unforgettably, that if you are Black in America, it does not matter who you are, racism will come knocking.... *Real American* is the story of that insidious harm and of a woman who became alert to the American racism within herself and fought back. *Real American* is not only an excellent, satisfying read but a book that can help us 'stay woke'—as we must—to the sometimes stealthy and always life-threatening danger of racism, so that we all can fight back."

—**Barbara Lee, U.S. representative and author of *Renegade for Peace and Justice: A Memoir of Political and Personal Courage***

REAL AMERICAN

ALSO BY JULIE LYTHCOTT-HAIMS

How to Raise an Adult

REAL AMERICAN

---

a memoir

JULIE LYTHCOTT-HAIMS

ST. MARTIN'S GRIFFIN NEW YORK

www.stmartins.com

The Library of Congress has cataloged the Henry Holt edition as follows:

Names: Lythcott-Haims, Julie, author.
Title: Real American : a memoir / Julie Lythcott-Haims.
Description: First edition. | New York, New York : Henry Holt and Company, 2017.
Identifiers: LCCN 2017009272 | ISBN 9781250137746 (hardcover) | ISBN 9781250137753 (ebook)
Subjects: LCSH: Lythcott-Haims, Julie. | Racially mixed people—United States—Biography. | Racially mixed people—Race identity—United States. | Racially mixed people—United States—Social conditions. | Race—Social aspects—United States. | United States—Race relations. | New York (N.Y.)—Biography. | Reston (Va.)—Biography. | Palo Alto (Ca.)—Biography. | Stanford (Ca.)—Biography.
Classification: LCC E184.A1 L967 2017 | DDC 305.800973—dc23
LC record available at https://lccn.loc.gov/2017009272

ISBN 978-1-250-29673-3 (trade paperback)

Our books may be purchased in bulk for promotional, educational, or business use. Please contact your local bookseller or the Macmillan Corporate and Premium Sales Department at 1-800-221-7945, extension 5442, or by email at MacmillanSpecialMarkets@macmillan.com.

First published by Henry Holt and Company

First St. Martin's Griffin Edition: August 2018

10 9 8 7 6 5

for Silvey, for whom Eden was no garden

CONTENTS

IT BEGINS LIKE THIS

I.

"Where are you from?"
"Here."
"No, I mean, where are you *from* from?"

As a child growing up in the seventies and early eighties in New York, Wisconsin, and Northern Virginia, there was something about my skin color and hair texture that snagged the attention of white children and adults. Their need to make sense of me—to make something of sense out of nonsensical me—was pressing. My existence was a ripple in an otherwise smooth sheet. They needed to iron it down.

[The truth is, I'm not really from here.]
[The truth is, that's not what they were asking.]

II.

The truth is, they were asking, "Why are you so different from what I know? So unclassifiable?"

There's love at first sight. There's *American at first sight*. And from dozens of "where are you from" interactions with Americans over the years, I've learned that *American at first sight* is about looks—primarily skin color and hair texture—not nationality.

I am the wooly-haired, medium-brown-skinned offspring typical when Blacks and whites have sex, which was considered illegal activity in seventeen of the fifty "united" states in 1966.

Nineteen sixty-six was the year before the U.S. Supreme Court decided in *Loving v. Virginia* that the laws preventing interracial marriage were unconstitutional, and 1966 was the year in which my Black father and white mother, an African American doctor and a British teacher who met in West Africa, chose to go ahead and get married anyway. They married in Accra, Ghana. I was born to them in Lagos, Nigeria, in 1967.

I come from people who broke the rules. Chose to live lives outside the box. Chose hope over hate as the arc of history was forced to bend a bit more toward justice. I am the goo in the melting pot.

Rhetorically championed.
Theoretically accepted.
Actually suspect.
In places hated.
Despised.

III.

In the lead-up to the 2008 presidential election a persona stepped to the forefront of public consciousness, that of the "Real American."

More than an individual you want to have a beer with, more than the everyman "Joe the Plumber," the "Real American" is code for an entire era when men like Andy Griffith ran Mayberry or John Wayne swaggered through a western town. When white men cloaked in clothes of real or perceived authority could take what they believed was rightfully theirs with an air of ownership to the opportunity, to the land, to the people, and of belonging at the center of the situation, whatever it was. A time when the word "he" meant all genders. When "normal" and "regular" meant "white."

This fictional character—the Real American—became a talisman, a lifeline to a more halcyon past for some white men and women bewildered by capitalism's demand for low-paid laborers and by the rising tide of legal and regulatory equality that dared to lift others' boats. They looked around at us the others knocking at the door of the hiring manager, the landlord, the admissions dean, the local restaurant. Looked frantically around and began to see fewer— less—of themselves.

Nursed by a milk of white supremacy fed to them as what was natural, right, and good for them, these whites believed the rest of us were interlopers, thieves at the door, threatening to take what was not ours. They grew incensed at the growing number of us others who refused to accept our place at the bottom of America's ladder underneath even the most lowly of whites.

These "Real Americans" found a voice in their candidates, grew in number, became a mob who raised slogans, signs, fists, and arms. Who long to make America great—

normal
regular
white

again.

IV.

These newly emboldened "Real Americans" issue angry orders to the rest of us: "If you don't like it, go back to where you came from."

There is no back to where I came from.

You stole my homeland from me.
Me from my homeland, I mean.
I don't even know where it is.
Literally.

V.

I came from Silvey.

I am the untallied, unpaid, unrepented damages of one of America's founding crimes. I come from people who endured the psycho-cultural genocide of slavery, reconstruction, and Jim Crow. Who began to find a place here really only quite recently amid strides toward effecting a more perfect union, of liberty and justice for all.

I am Silvey's great-great-great-great-granddaughter. She was a slave who worked on a plantation in the late 1700s in Charleston, South Carolina, the harbor town through which close to one in two African slaves entered America over the centuries. Silvey bore three children by her master, Joshua Eden, by which I mean he raped her; there is no consent in slavery. Silvey's daughter Silvia was born in 1785, and Joshua freed Silvey, Silvia, and their other children some years later. Silvia gave birth to a son named Joshua in 1810. Joshua had a son named Joshua Jr., born in 1845. His daughter, Evelyn, was born in 1896. Evelyn bore my father, George, in 1918. And I was born to him in 1967.

The original Americans are the natives whose land was invaded then stolen by the Europeans. Those descended from the Europeans, the ones who came on ships to the New World, like to think they are the original Americans. But I'm from a third set—from those brought here on different ships over different waters, those whose sweat and muscle were the engine of the American economy for over two hundred years, whose blood and tears watered America's ground. I come from them.

I come from people who survived what America did to them.

Ain't I a Real American?

VI.

When the amorphous mob harrumphs about the needs and rights of "Real Americans," they don't picture me. People like me. But is anyone more a product of America than those of us formed by America in an angry war with herself?

This is rhetorical. Theoretical. Of course we are not *more* than. We're *less* than, not even equal to. The remainder of an imperfect equation. The child who wasn't supposed to exist. The undesired other. The bastard child of illegitimate rules who dares even to *be*.

The contradiction of being "less than" in a nation whose forming documents speak of liberty and justice for all plagued me for much of my young adult life.

I'm so American it hurts.

AN AMERICAN CHILDHOOD

I.

As a child growing up in the 1970s, I adored my country, as I imagine most American children do.

When I was three we moved from our Manhattan apartment to a rickety eighteenth-century house my parents rented in an old hamlet known as Snedens Landing in the town of Palisades, New York. Snedens is tucked into the western bank of the Hudson River across from Manhattan and farther north. Its homes nestle along the main road, Washington Spring Road, which meanders through town, then makes a steep, winding descent to the Hudson River below. Alongside the main road and through the backyards of some of the houses runs a stream—the spring said to have provided respite to General George Washington and his troops in 1780, while the nearby woods gave cover to the traitor Benedict Arnold. When the Revolutionary War ended at the Battle of Yorktown in 1781, the British warship HMS *Perseverance* sailed across the Hudson over to Snedens Landing and fired a seventeen-gun salute in recognition of the brand-new country, the United States of America. Our tiny rented house dated back to these times and, clinging to the hillside, rather looked like an old man, groaning, with an aching back, weathered by weather and time.

By the time I was five my parents had scrounged together enough money to buy a house, this one further up the street on Washington Spring Road, of 1950s modern design, with large living-room windows that looked out at the creek below and onto the thick woods beyond. As a small child I played in that creek with my friend Conrad, a little white boy whose name I mispronounced as "Comrade." Conrad and I would launch leaf and stick boats into the creek, which couldn't have been more than two feet across and three or four inches deep, and then we'd watch delighted and wide-eyed as the current took our little creations down and away and ultimately beyond our sight. I recall feeling a strong pang of worry and hope over whether my little boats would be all right. If they'd get caught up in an eddy or a beaver's dam, get sidetracked and end up on the muddy brown creek bank, or maybe make it to an enormous freedom in the famous river below. That backyard stream was a wonderful laboratory for me and Conrad. One afternoon I lowered my underpants and squatted over the gently flowing water, then stood back with tremendous satisfaction at proving Conrad wrong: poop sinks.

I marched in a Fourth of July parade in Palisades when I was six, my large Afro distinctive among my group of straight-haired peers and adults. I was sporting my Brownie jumper and sash, with its little "Girl Scouts U.S.A." patch stitched in white letters at the top. I drew up my spine and straightened my neck at the honor of wearing that uniform to march with my troop past our town's tiny post office, while our neighbors held ice-cream cones and applauded from the side of the road.

Palisades was where I memorized my first phone numbers, my first address and zip code. As a student at Palisades Elementary School, I jumped to my feet for the Pledge of Allegiance and sang all of the patriotic songs with gusto. My favorites were "This Land Is Your Land," because it contained the name of my state, New York, and "The Star-Spangled Banner," for its unabashedly triumphant violence. On field day at the end of second grade, I ran the fifty-yard dash, and even though I ran diagonally across the field instead of straight ahead I came in third out of twenty and got a lovely little bronze medal the size of a quarter.

When I was seven, my father's growing prominence in the field of public health and academic medicine spurred his departure from the faculty of Columbia University. He moved us to Madison, Wisconsin; he would be Associate Vice Chancellor for Health Services at the University there. It was 1975. Third-grade math was taught by a stern woman named Mrs. Bernard, my first African American teacher, and I took to memorizing my multiplication tables like it was a game I had to win, and did. The following summer I recall the hard work of weaving red, white, and blue streamers through the back and front wheels of my ten-speed bicycle in honor of our nation's Bicentennial. Riding that bicycle in the parade wending through my tree-lined neighborhood, Arbor Hills, in Madison, I felt important, giddy, alive.

A year later we moved to Reston, Virginia, a planned community located just outside of Washington, D.C., boasting a sort of utopian commitment to racial and socioeconomic diversity. President Jimmy Carter had appointed Daddy to be his Assistant Surgeon General with responsibility for running the Health Services Administration in the Department of Health, Education, and Welfare. It was 1977.

On a school field trip to our nation's capital with my fifth-grade classmates, I felt a swell of admiration for America and a surge of pride to be American as I stared up at the gleaming white Washington Monument, heard my voice echo as I walked around Lincoln in his chair, traced my fingers over the bronze plaques. We walked back to our bus in a gaggle and for a few moments were caught in the jumble of people in their gray trench coats trying to hurry down sidewalks to and from their jobs. I stepped to the side so they could pass. Important people worked in this city. I knew my Daddy was one of them.

Back at home in Reston, I had Black friends, Indian friends, and Jewish friends, as well as white friends. There was even another Black family on my street for the very first time in my life, with a daughter named Amanda. Amanda was a few years younger than me, but we could both sense that it was very important to our parents that we become friends. And we did become friends, genuinely, telling each other our secrets, playing board games, and sequestering ourselves behind locked doors to review the girlie magazines our fathers thought they kept well hidden. I felt a mix of wonder and awe as we pawed through page spreads of creamy white skin.

Over the years I did extremely well in school, was a student government representative, sold Girl Scout cookies, and tied a thick yellow ribbon to the strong tree that stood at our curb in honor of the American hostages in Iran.

III.

I adored Daddy. He was fifty when I was born and my childhood coincided with the heyday of his career, which began against all odds amidst the racial hatred of the segregated Jim Crow South. I was his last child of five—the product of his second marriage to my mother— and I knew from the way his eyes twinkled whenever he looked at me that he loved me no matter what. He gave me a variety of nicknames— Old Sport, Knuckle Head—which sounds crude to my grown ears but then, spoken in the butter of his baritone, it felt like melted love. He never had to call for me twice. I came running every single time.

When I was little and skinned my knee, he'd pull me up onto his tall lap, kiss me, and ask with all seriousness how I was going to become Miss America with that scar. I didn't know then that no Black woman had yet been crowned Miss America and that no Black woman would be crowned Miss America until 1983. Instead I heard in Daddy's words that I was beautiful, perhaps the most beautiful girl he'd ever seen.

We all called him "Daddy," even my mother. He was formidable, commanding, gruff, loving, and funny. I hung on to his every word, whether it was "Baby, bring me my cigarettes," or a well-placed retort to the news recited by the anchorman on TV.

Daddy was the protagonist, the lead.

Daddy was the sun.

IV.

Beauty pageants weren't my thing, though. I wanted to be something more like President.

By the end of my junior year in high school (by which time we were back in Wisconsin), I'd been elected vice president of my class for the third year in a row, and in the fall of my senior year, the student council elected me president of that governing body. I was selected for "Badger Girls State"—a statewide program for kids interested in policy and politics held the summer after high school graduation, and was elected senator there. I went on to be one of four presidents of my class at Stanford University, and one of four elected class leaders of my graduating class at Harvard Law School.

I was on track to live the American Dream—through hard work, big dreams, and a bit of luck, to become whoever I wanted.

Mine was in many ways a very American childhood. And, with the buttress of money and influence that came from my father's professional success, it was also a childhood of material comfort that set me up for a privileged life.

BECOMING THE OTHER

I.

Daddy never liked the Fourth of July.

I couldn't understand it, because I adored the parades, songs, and flags, the neighborhood barbecues, the explosion of firecrackers, and the smart looks on everyone's faces that revealed the innate understanding that our country was better—and by extension we the people were better—than the rest of the world.

My mother was the one to inform me of Daddy's opinion about the Fourth, and she did so in a whispered-sideways-glance kind of way with no explanation as to why he felt it. I understood from the way she said it that it had something to do with Daddy's past, his experiences, his Blackness. Her silent "why" bespoke pain too painful to discuss, so I never asked. Didn't think it related to the America I was inhabiting anyway. Didn't think I was Black in the ways he was. Thought America was beyond all that.

I was wrong.

Looking back over the years of even my earliest childhood, the clues were everywhere.

II

Back in Snedens Landing, I'd begun to sense that something might be wrong with people with dark skin. I lacked the language to describe it and the intellect to analyze it, but I felt the chill of it in my bones, the red-hot heat of it surging up the back of my neck when I was out and about with Daddy.

Daddy was six foot two and lean, with a neat, tightly coiled Afro he kept supple with Afro Sheen, and skin that was dark and crinkly like the top layer of a brownie. On those occasional weekend days when he wasn't traveling or busy at the desk in his den, he'd take me with him on an errand in town, and every now and then to an event in Manhattan. Holding his hand walking down the local street or a bustling city sidewalk, I noticed that some strangers stared at him with eyes that steamed like a cauldron, as if they could brand him like an animal with their searing focus if he dared to look them in the eye. I'd look up at my tall daddy for reassurance, pleading with my small brown eyes to know what was going on, but he gripped my hand tighter, kept his eyes focused straight ahead, pursed his lips tight, and kept walking.

When I walked down the same streets with my white mother, nobody steamed at her that way. The glances she got as a white woman holding the tiny hand of a small brown child were far more subtle. It took a lot longer for me to discern and label those looks as pity and disdain. By choosing to marry my father, she'd crossed a line. By choosing to have me.

III.

I was learning that something might be wrong with me.

I began kindergarten as a four-year-old who would turn five in November. And that year, or maybe it was first grade, I began coming home with my classmates' questions: "What *are* you?" and "*She's* your mother?"

When I mentioned these comments to my parents, they responded with all the vociferousness and passion of a political advocacy campaign that I was "Black." It was a deliberate strategy—almost a strategic plan, I could tell—because they'd land heavy glances on each other as they said these things to me. Later I'd learn it's what parents of mixed kids did in the 1970s; there was then no widespread use of the concept "multiracial" or "biracial," and the ill-fated term "mulatto" going back to slave days, denoting the half-and-half mixture of slaves and whites, was considered in poor taste. "Call mixed kids Black," the thinking went, "because the world will see and treat them as Black. They'd better claim it and be proud of it. They'd better know how to defend it. How to hold their heads high. Be Black and proud."

I was not privy to the sociopolitical agenda. I was just bewildered.

Why was I the race of one parent and not the other, effectively denying my mother's contribution to my loosely curling Afro and brown-paper-bag-colored skin that made me look so different from almost everyone else I encountered, including both of my parents as well as my half siblings from Daddy's first marriage to a woman who was half Black Cape Verdean and half White Cape Verdean (from the Portuguese who colonized the island), who'd given my half siblings more easily discernible Black features?

And given the choice between white and Black, why were my parents adamant about labeling me the race that so many people seemed to find problematic? In forcing this "Black" label on me and even bringing it on herself, why was my white mother choosing to lower herself into this pit instead of using her whiteness to lift me and Daddy up and out of it?

IV.

Mom was the Blackest white lady I knew. Maybe even the Blackest person I knew.

Daddy was so immersed in his work and international travel that he was for many months over many years more of a ghostly figure, an absent presence in our daily life. His other children, my siblings, were a generation older than I was, and when they popped in and out of our home for the holidays and an occasional weekend visit, I loved being around them, their enormous Afros, their raucous laughter over stories laced with innuendo that made my mother raise her eyebrows. But I would not come to know them deeply until I was an adult myself. Mom was the one who shouldered the enormous task of bringing Blackness to light.

Born in England, Mom had lived in West Africa for seven years in her twenties, which is where she'd met Daddy, and she'd become a naturalized American citizen in 1968 with white skin tanned a copper brown. She wore dresses made of cloth she'd bought in Nigeria, which made white friends and neighbors here in New York raise their eyebrows, as if she was maybe affiliated with Black activist groups, maybe even the Black Panthers.

She'd read the research that said that Black children need Black dolls to help develop a healthy psychological self. So she filled my childhood bedroom with those dolls, and also read me texts by Black authors, like Nikki Giovanni's poetry collection, *Spin a Soft Black Song*. She knew the prominent Black thinkers and artists of the time, and could pronounce names like Ntozake Shange accurately and with a little flair, maybe even gusto, like she enjoyed how it felt to make those sounds with her lips and tongue, sounds that prompted bewilderment in other white adults. My mother even went so far as to deny her ethnic ancestry by saying to strangers—such as the white Mormon missionaries who knocked on our door in Snedens Landing in 1975 when I was seven—"Sorry, you have nothing for us. We are a Black family." The missionaries agreed with her and turned away.

I could tell she was putting on an act. Her actions a costume worn by a character in a play designed to transport us to a different reality. But I wasn't transported. I was annoyed. I could see she was trying too hard to convince herself, the world, and me.

One day when I was about six she came home with two picture books she'd bought at a local store. In these days before the "playdate" I had a friend over without her knowing it, and, not wanting to be rude to my friend, my mother acted as if she'd planned all along that one of the books was for my friend and the other for me. My friend and I had immediately reached out for the same book, the one whose cover featured an animal of some kind. As we tugged over who would get that book, my mother gently said the second book was for me. It was *The Snowy Day* by Ezra Jack Keats, and the drawing on its cover was of a Black child. Why? Why did I have to read those books if my friend, who was white, didn't? Couldn't I have those white dolls my friends had? Didn't we all know they were the more beautiful dolls, those with the bluest of eyes? Wasn't I good enough for those white dolls? Those white books? Wasn't I good enough for the white world?

I would physically bristle when my mother referred to "us" as a "Black family." She seemed to be trying to join a club it seemed rational to want to leave. But so long as I was in it, I wanted to keep out anyone who lacked the chops to belong. I'd fume silently every time she said it, and when she was out of view I rolled my little dark brown eyes.

V.

Of all her efforts to raise a Black daughter well, the most confounding and persistent challenge for my mother was my hair. No matter how Black she tried to be, when it came to my hair she was a stranger in a strange land.

With no one else around to look to for guidance, my hair was a mystery to me as well.

I did not learn for decades that hair is a psychological barometer for Black girls and women—it's alternately our pride or the bane of our existence as we try to locate a sense of self within Western norms of beauty, respond to definitions of "neat and tidy" and "professional," and bear up under humid weather.

I had an Afro of loose brown curls until I was about eight when I decided to grow my hair long enough so that it could be pulled back, reined in, tamped down. In fourth grade in Madison, Wisconsin, I'd sit before the large mirror in my bedroom day after day, and Mom would stand behind me holding a brush like a wizard brandishing a new wand, her eyes round in frightened wonder anticipating both the potential and the disasters that were possible. Stroke by stroke she'd pull my pile of frizz into a ponytail and secure it tight with an elastic holder, the kind with little plastic bobbles that allowed you to wrap the hair tight with the elastic and then use the bobbles to secure one end of the tie to the other. She didn't know the importance of gels and creams and other Black hair care products, so the hair of the ponytail was a frizzy ball of puff.

I grew older. We moved to Reston, Virginia. My hair was an immediate demarcation of difference between me and my friends, me and the magazine image of beautiful, me and normal. From television I knew that Black girls straightened their hair chemically, but my father forbade my mother from doing that to my hair because of the extreme damage he saw done to girls' hair in his youth five decades earlier. I pleaded that today's products were different. But he would hear none of it, and Daddy's word was all but law. Mom had to choose her battles and this was not going be one of them; even if Daddy's perspective was decades out of date, he held the trump card on any conversation related to Blackness. So I used a curling iron to help smooth my hair to make it look more like I felt I should look. The way I wanted to look. More like the hair I saw on Black girls on TV and more like my white friends. Mom would sit with me as I tried to turn my frizzy hair into some kind of smooth, swoopy, flippy design. But it just wouldn't lie flat or flip backward like the hair of Farrah Fawcett, the actress and pinup girl with super hair all my white friends tried to imitate with varying degrees of success. The best I could do was smooth my hair into a longer, sleeker ponytail. I began to use the curling iron every day.

Over time, these efforts to smooth and constrain my hair took their toll. When I was eleven and in sixth grade, the hair at the back of my head began to break off from the damage done by the taut rubber hair ties that held the ponytail. Toward the end of that school year, Mom took me to her hairdresser, a Black woman named Angie, to see what could be done. As I sat in the big vinyl barber's chair and looked in the mirror at all the implements and instruments of beauty in the store, Angie and Mom spoke in conspiratorial tones off to the side and behind me. *About* me. When it was time to begin the cut, Angie swiveled the chair so my back was to the mirror, then proceeded to cut. All I could see was my mother looking on, pleased. When Angie was done she spun me around to look at my new self in the mirror and I stifled a horrified cry upon seeing the very short Afro that blanketed my head. I was embarrassed to be embarrassed to be wearing the traditional hair of my people, yet I felt as if I'd been assaulted. The next day we had a car wash fund-raiser at my elementary school, and although my tiny breasts were starting to push against my shirt fabric a customer mistook me for a boy.

VI.

In fifth grade at Lake Anne Elementary School in Reston, Virginia, one of my white friends got pulled into the gifted and talented group. She was smart but no smarter than I was, I knew. And now she was getting to do cool projects and puzzles but not me? I went home and mentioned it to my mom, who came to meet with my teacher, Mr. Pulansky, a few days later. Pulansky was not persuaded. So my Mom escalated to the principal, this time insisting that I be tested. They brought in someone from the district to give me an IQ test. Mailed the results to our house. Mom thought I wasn't watching when she opened the envelope, read the results, and squirreled the letter away in a drawer.

I was put in the gifted group soon after and shortly after that Mr. Pulansky announced to our entire class, "Apparently, all it takes to be gifted is for your parent to meet with the principal." But in the privacy of an afternoon home alone, I'd peeked at the letter from the district. The raw score was 99th percentile. As my teacher stood smug at the front of the classroom, it was the first time in my young life I uttered a very silent *fuck you.*

VII.

Junior high was a game changer. A big school with students from many surrounding towns and an instant infusion of Black kids. LaVerne was a head taller and more developed than the rest in our group, and was dark skinned and strong. She had an opinion on all kinds of things from dating to politics, and a quick tongue when challenged. I admired her. More than that, I yearned for more of her—she, this physical clue to how I might look and behave one day. We both went out for track, and I was fast. LaVerne took notice and gave me a huge hug after my 2:28 time in the 880-yard run. I didn't know then that Daddy had been a great runner in college. I'm not even sure he knew that I had taken up running myself.

At Daddy's urging, Mom signed us up for Jack and Jill, the social organization for middle-class Black families founded in the 1930s when most American Boy and Girl Scout troops refused to let Blacks in. Each J&J family took turns hosting the monthly meetings. When it came time for our turn and Mom and I were setting out plates and napkins and arranging hors d'oeuvres on the buffet table, I was apprehensive over whether our guests would feel we were living the right kind of Black life.

The doorbell began to ring. As I took coats and led people downstairs, I saw parents nod to one another at the paintings in the foyer done by African artists and point to the large wall hanging on the circular stairway as they made their way down into the living room. I overheard Mom answering questions about the sculptures standing in the living-room corners, the figurines on table tops and in bookshelves. I saw people run their finger slowly over the carved ivory tusk that sat on the bookshelf along the far wall. The meeting came and went and, as secretary, I recorded the minutes. When the night was over I'd learned that the artifacts my parents amassed over their seven years in West Africa were an exquisite mask that communicated, particularly to Black adults, that our family was in fact quite Black. Our African art helped us seem more Black American. I had a nagging feeling we were less than we seemed.

Toward the end of seventh grade, LaVerne convinced me and another girl to do a dance in the talent show portion of the upcoming Jack and Jill annual gala. LaVerne choreographed it and she and I practiced over back-to-back weekends, with LaVerne always pointing out where the third girl would go. When the big evening came, both Mom and Daddy were there. Daddy looked out of place mingling with parents he did not know. His being there was Mom's doing, I knew, because his face was reluctant but resigned to the fact of it, like when you roll up your sleeves for a shot at the doctor's office.

When it came time for the talent show portion of the evening, about fifty parents and other family members gathered, and my parents seated themselves in the metal chairs three rows back from the empty space at the front of the room that was our makeshift stage. I stood on the sidelines nervously awaiting our group's turn. We started out fine, but halfway through the song I forgot the steps and looked out of the side of my eye at LaVerne to pantomime what she was doing. I couldn't remember and couldn't recover. I stumbled off to the side and stood there holding my arms against my chest, rocking side to side on my heels, staring at LaVerne and the other girl so as to avoid eye contact with anyone else. It was just a dance, and soon it was over. But it felt like an omen.

On November 4, 1980, I was in eighth grade and about to turn thirteen. It was Election Day, a Tuesday, and that evening I was babysitting someone's kid. As the election results came in, I watched with deepening worry the news of Ronald Reagan's apparent landslide victory over President Carter. I knew this meant my father would lose his job. I knew this meant we'd move. Somewhere. But I didn't know that I'd be saying good-bye to Black friends for a long, long time. And I didn't know how much that would matter.

I would live in eight homes before going off to college, the only child in a very traditionally gendered household of high academic expectations. Moving frequently made me good at conveying myself to others so as to be accepted. But I never really learned to stop trying hard to be whoever they wanted me to be and just be.

In the spring of that final year of living in Northern Virginia, the Jack and Jill adults threw an evening dance party at a fancy hotel for us thirteen- and fourteen-year-olds. I wore the new magenta jewel-toned velour top and Calvin Klein jeans I'd gotten for Christmas, put on the small bit of makeup my mother would allow, and smoothed and curled my hair in a way that looked pretty good. I felt beautiful as I walked into the party, but tentative. I was worried about whether I could dance well enough to blend in.

When the DJ started playing, a few girls and boys began dancing right away, and then more, and then most. But I hung back on the edge of the parquet dance floor, moving my hips and shoulders ever so gently to the thudding disco and R&B music, wanting to be dancing, wanting to feel what my body might do in response to these beats and rhythms, wanting to relax and have fun like all these other kids seemed to be doing, but not wanting to draw attention to myself.

After about twenty minutes, a boy who'd been at the center of the dancers out on the floor broke away from the others and came toward me, kind of dancing as he walked and smiling broadly. He reached for my hand. I felt suddenly shy, which was a feeling I was not accustomed to. I could feel the strong thud of my heart in my chest. I pulled back and shook my head no. He beckoned with his chin, still holding out his hand. Chosen. I was chosen. Was this really happening?

This boy was beautiful, and I knew from our J&J meetings over these past few years that he was kind. But we'd never really spoken. I stepped forward and walked out onto the dance floor behind him. The boy—I don't recall his name, *wish I could recall his name*—had moves that were three and four times beyond what everyone else had going on, but I just tried to copy what everyone else was doing. He stayed with me. Danced with me. Around me. Kept returning to me with his smiling eyes. Finally I returned his gaze and held it. The song was "Good Times" and when I stopped thinking so hard, my body just did what it wanted to do, which was dance. The DJ put on "Rapper's Delight" next. When that long song was over, I shouted to my new friend, "How'd you learn to dance so well?" "Awww," he replied with his beautiful huge smile. Then he spun away from me to do a signature move. "My Mama taught me."

Following Reagan's victory came the routine dismissal of all the previous president's appointees, including my father. By January 1981, Daddy had decided to return us to Wisconsin where he'd take a high-level administrative position at the medical school at the University of Wisconsin–Madison and resume a part-time pediatric practice there.

My parents might have chosen to buy a home in the vibrant, multicultural capital city of Madison, a real city with people from all over the world, as is the hallmark of any university town. Instead they bought the larger plot of land and nicer house their affluence made possible in a development west of Madison in the town of Verona. The development was called Cherrywood—a bit of wishful thinking. It was actually surrounded on all sides by cornfields and had a middle-of-nowhere feel to it.

We moved to Cherrywood in the summer of 1981 and soon met our across-the-street neighbors, the Sullivans, a family of kind white folk originally from rural Vermont with a grown child living back in New England and a younger child named Lisa who was then ten. Unlike both of my parents, neither Mr. nor Mrs. Sullivan was college educated. Mr. Sullivan had worked his way into senior management in the food industry. He'd recently been made president of a company headquartered in Madison and they'd moved to Cherrywood just months before we had. Despite the fact that I was thirteen and headed off to high school, and Lisa was only ten and still in elementary school, we bonded over being outsiders, lonely, and new. Our parents also quickly became fast friends and over the years would become true confidants, dear to each other. They cherished the improbability of being neighbors in the first place, let alone folks who genuinely liked each other.

One weekend evening when we'd lived there about a year, as our fathers fussed over the barbecue in Lisa's backyard and our mothers made side dishes in the kitchen, Lisa and I were upstairs in her small bedroom, sprawled out on her carpeted floor, reading a teen magazine. When we finished leafing through the glossy pages, I smelled dinner penetrating the stale air of the bedroom and suddenly felt very hungry. I rolled over, got up, and headed for the door when Lisa began to speak.

"I'm not supposed to tell you this—"
I paused and turned around. "What?"

"My sister was visiting when you guys first moved here. She saw your dad across the street on his riding lawn mower and said, 'Oooh look, they have a Black gardener.'"

For a split second I stared at Lisa lying there on the floor, my eyes wide, my breath clenched in my throat. Then I shifted my gaze up toward the far wall, keeping my body as still as possible, as if a bad smell had arisen from her and if I just didn't move at all, didn't disturb the air between us, the smell wouldn't come any closer to me. Through her bedroom window I could see a portion of our lawn, large, green, and plush, across the bucolic street.

Daddy loves riding that mower, I thought to myself. Steps on the running board with his left foot and swings that bent right leg over and around, like getting on the back of a horse. He's so proud to have all of this land, these lawns, so excited to think ahead to next spring's gardens. My parents would take a stroll around the property every night, cocktails in hand, admiring the *gardenia*—Daddy's favorite flower—that grew near the back door, pointing to where the tulips would come up after the cold winter, checking on the three pines they'd planted to give the lawn a bit of character. Our house was bigger than the Sullivans'. My father was the fucking former Assistant Surgeon General of the God Damn United States. I took a deep breath and cocked my head back toward Lisa, who still lay on the floor.

"Swear you won't tell?" she asked. Then she scrambled to stand up. "My parents made me promise not to tell you."

I nodded slightly as if in a trance, feeling the heat rise up my neck. I looked to the walls of Lisa's small bedroom, to the photos of a Vermont childhood tacked up above her desk.

"C'mon," I said, turning toward the bedroom door and opening it. I walked out of her room and strode down the hallway to the stairs that led to the kitchen. I could hear Lisa calling out, her voice sputtering, could hear her footsteps as she scrambled to catch up with me. I smiled at this satisfying feeling, this small bit of control I had in this moment, this choice I had, this chance to say something, and what, or to say nothing at all, as I made my way toward our four parents.

"You have to promise," I heard her say from the stairs, as I reached the kitchen.
"Promise what?" Lisa's mother asked.
"Nothing." I forced a smile, picturing this small-town Vermont family

having their secret conversation about mine. The mothers glanced at each other.

I grabbed a bowl of potato salad in one hand and the green salad in the other, and edged my way through the partially open screen door leading to the backyard. I plunked the food on the picnic table on the small patio, then found a place at the end of one bench and sat. I took in the sight of the salads, the hot dogs and burgers, fruit, beers and sodas, the bottles of ketchup and mustard, the freshly picked corn. I listened to the sound of adults in easy conversation, relaxing into their strengthening friendship. My stomach grumbled. I took a cheeseburger and began to eat it, and worked hard to keep my feelings to myself.

I was embarrassed for Daddy, who took such pride in mowing the gorgeous lawn at the large home he'd worked so hard to provide for us. Embarrassed for the Sullivans that they'd had to have an uncomfortable conversation they thought they were keeping safely from us. Embarrassed for Lisa for being so naive—or just young—as to relay this story to me, as if revealing what her ignorant family member had said was a greater gift than keeping it to herself. And maybe it was. I took a bite of my burger, and then another, and another, and then a gulp of iced tea. I looked over at my smiling, innocent parents and was embarrassed, in a way, for all of us.

It was only natural that Lisa's big sister was confused seeing Daddy astride his tractor mower. Most Black people didn't own homes like this. Most Black people were more likely to be someone's gardener than a home owner in a community like this one, weren't they? I watched Mr. Sullivan pop open a can of Leinenkugel's and hand it to my father and then grab one for himself. They shared a hearty laugh over something they wanted to keep between themselves. Was I going to get Lisa in trouble for "telling" what we all knew was true—that Blacks tend to play roles of subservience to whites? No. It was the fact of the Sullivans whispering about it among themselves that made me feel most uncomfortable. I calmed that feeling by eating my burger. I felt safe knowing that none of the grown-ups knew what I knew.

IX.

When we moved to Cherrywood in the summer of 1981, I was an incoming high school freshman. The summer that we moved, my mother decided it was time for her to try to give me some braids, which she'd gleaned was how Black girls my age were supposed to wear their hair. She fashioned it French-style, in two big rows that marched down either side of my head. She still didn't know about the kinds of products that would tame and moisturize my hair—nor did I—so my braids looked like untended crops, a halo of unkempt hair springing up like kudzu around them.

I enrolled at Middleton High School, located one town over from Verona, which did not have its own high school. Middleton High had about twelve hundred other students, many of whom lived on farms in places far more remote than Cherrywood, most of whom had been in school together since kindergarten, and practically all of whom were white. Three of the student body were Black—me, and a pair of siblings who were a sophomore boy and senior girl, the children of the head coach of the University of Wisconsin men's basketball team. I never met the sister, but over the years I did exchange a few brief words with the brother.

I searched for familiar things. Three weeks into the school year I saw a poster announcing freshman class officer elections. I decided to run for class secretary—a role on the team, yet innocuous. A way to ease myself into things. It came time to give our speeches. The entire class of three hundred was in the gym, seated in the bleachers. I stood at the podium in red corduroy pants and a pink short-sleeved shirt with hair like a tumbleweed and began speaking into the mike. My classmates weren't quieting down, though. They kept chattering amongst themselves. I tapped the mike and got their attention. They quieted. "My name is Julie Lythcott," I began.

I came in second out of three vying for the post and one good that came of running was that I got to know people. A classmate named Diana befriended me. She was beautiful, kind, wore big glasses, and was easygoing, with a cursory interest in academics but very plugged in socially. Like a friendly clerk on Ellis Island who might actually take an interest in an immigrant's assimilation, she pulled me over the imaginary line demarcating who was outside and who was inside this new community by calling me at night to be sure we were dressing identically at school the next day, and by inviting me to the boy/girl parties she threw in her basement. She was my closest friend for four years and genuinely liked me for me. I wouldn't have made it through Middleton High School if it hadn't been for Diana.

In our ninth-grade U.S. history class, I felt only the briefest emotional stirring as I read the small paragraph our textbook devoted to slavery. No need to dwell on it. No need to examine it. It was behind us. This was 1981, after all.

Diana loved black-and-white movies depicting the Antebellum South, and often suggested that we watch them together. My intestines twisted at the thought of having to watch, but I couldn't articulate why.

X.

In the spring of my freshman year, I fell hard for a boy named Nick. His skin was practically paper white and covered with freckles, his legs were strong from playing soccer, and he was smart as hell and knew it. Our lockers sat right next to each other, and at the end of school one day, as we packed our backpacks before catching our bus home, we laughed about something that turned out to be so hilarious that we ended up falling to the floor with giggles. It would be common today for a friend to whip out a phone and photograph the moment, but in those days no one carried a camera. Our friend Jenny ran to her nearby locker to get the camera she kept there and came running back to me and Nick, still giggling on the floor. I can't remember what we were laughing about, but I remember feeling in that instant on that shiny cement floor that I was falling in love. Jenny had the film developed at the local drugstore and ordered prints for all three of us.

I pinned the photo to the corkboard on my bedroom wall. One day Daddy noticed it, looked over at me with a loving smile, then shook his head.

"White boys will be your friend," he said with his booming bass voice, "but they'll never date you."

I trembled. Neither then nor ever did I challenge Daddy's authority. His decision to move to this remote area. I never knew how to ask, *Why'd you move me to this all-white town?*

XI.

The summer after freshman year, I was fourteen, and Diana's aunt took us to a public swimming pool in a nearby town. As we walked along the cement in search of lounge chairs, a stranger going past us in the other direction stopped short, turned around, and said in that round, wide-mouthed, Midwestern twang, "*Oooooh mye gaaaaaaaaash. Uuuuure soh taaaaaaaan.*" I smiled and looked over at the kids splashing in the pool, not wanting to draw further attention to myself. I did not correct her.

XII.

I turned fifteen in the fall of my sophomore year. My hair was longer now, and once again I was straightening it with a curling iron and wearing it down for school pictures and other formal occasions. But I still knew nothing about hair products for Black girls, and however straight and neat my hair was when I left our house in Cherrywood, by midday the humidity in the air made it puff and frizz. On those days, Nick and the other boys I hung out with—the boys I fantasized about as I went to sleep each night—laughed in my face, pointed at my weird hair, and called me Bozo the Clown.

XIII.

I usually went along when Mom went grocery shopping at Cub Foods. The two of us would stand there at the checkout, across the black conveyor belt from the cashier, across the black conveyor belt that contained the groceries for our family, and occasionally, unpredictably, the cashier, whoever it was, would make eye contact with my mother and place his hand on that black conveyor belt wherever there was a discernible gap between one item and the next, trying to demarcate which groceries were hers and which were mine.

"This'll be it for you?"

"No, it's all of this. We're together."

My mom speaking as the eyes of the clerk tell me I cannot possibly belong to my own mother.

XIV.

There was only one Jewish kid at my school: Rachel Klein. Her Dad, Dr. Jacob Klein, was also a physician, and he shared a pediatric practice with Daddy at the university. In a twist of Midwestern irony, here were the Black and the Jew, persecuted throughout history yet rising above in Madison, Wisconsin.

Rachel was one year older than I was and also a member of our school's choir, which was consistently regarded as the very best choir in the state. In the fall of my sophomore year as the holidays approached, Rachel and her parents got themselves in a heap of trouble when they complained to our choir director about the Christian themes at the heart of every single choir song. Our director would have none of it, so the Kleins complained to the school administration, and ultimately to the school board. The result was that our director was forced to include one non-Christian song in each show from then on. Every time we got out the sheet music to rehearse "Ya Ba Bom," a Jewish folk song, our director would glare at Rachel.

I didn't really understand the Kleins' concern. The Christian music was exquisitely beautiful. All great choirs sang it. We were a great choir. Why did they have to try to ruin things for the rest of us?

I didn't yet know about allies. That Rachel needed one. That I'd need allies of my own one day. That maybe I even needed some allies right there and then.

XV.

I spent a lot of time at Diana's house and she at mine. One day during sophomore year when I'd gone over to her house to hang out, I found her in the basement rec room watching a movie on her VCR. It was *Gone with the Wind*. She looked up at me and said hello, then she turned her gaze back to the television screen and sighed like a Southern belle.

"Wouldn't it have been great to live back then?"
"No?"
"Why not?"
"Because I would have been a slave."
"Oh, but I mean if you weren't Black."
"But I am Black."
"I don't think of you as Black. I think of you as normal."

XVI.

I knew what Diana meant. I felt very un-Black myself, even as my parents continued to insist I was Black, even as I tried to figure out what that meant and to be that person in this white town.

The only Black people I saw on any regular basis were members of my own family—my father and my four siblings who were now in their mid- to late thirties and had lives and families of their own. Like anyone in America, I was bombarded with negative media portrayal and stereotypes about Blacks. And those negative images helped me construct a sense of self.

From *The Jeffersons*, *All in the Family*, and *Good Times*, I knew that Black people seemed to be someone's edgy, hip, funny friend who spoke in some kind of special jargon, who seemed either athletic, or to know how to dance well, or to be lazy, and who greeted other Blacks with a special handshake. From the news, I knew we were associated with poverty and crime. With my parents' constant refrain about me being Black, I thought it was on me to be a great dancer, do my best not to appear to be lazy or badly behaved, and figure out that handshake.

While I was trying to construct this Black self in a completely white world, one day I overheard my mother talking to my visiting sister who was in her late thirties. "I wish Julie had more Black friends," my mother said, sighing. I felt judged. Blamed even. Where was I to find Black friends in an all-white town? Did my own mother think I was prejudiced against Black people?

Was I?

She couldn't have been blaming me, I now know. She was likely blaming herself, her inability to stand up to Daddy who made all the important decisions in our family life such as where we would live. Mom knew I needed Black friends and was confiding in my sister about it. But I was already feeling recalcitrant toward Blackness and my place in it. I heard in my mother's words criticism that maybe I was avoiding Blacks on purpose. I heard in my mother's words my own criticism of my self.

XVII.

When spring of my sophomore year came around, my classmates started making noises about junior prom, a ritual open to all grades at our school despite its name. A few weeks before the dance I got wind that a senior named Rob was thinking of asking me. I knew Rob from choir. He was kind, and smart-boy witty. In a school where choral music was not just appreciated but championed, we all revered the very mature bass voice and heart he brought to his solo in "Swing Low, Sweet Chariot."

But Daddy's admonition clanged like a warning bell in my ears: "White boys will be your friend but they'll never date you." *Is Rob so far down the pecking order of white boys that he can't find a single white girl to date? Is something wrong with him? Is he settling for me?*

I panicked. I'd been raised to think well of myself. I didn't want to go to the prom as someone's consolation prize.

I decided to prevent that from happening by inviting someone to the prom myself—not a boy I had a crush on; someone who couldn't say no on the basis of race. There was that one Black boy in our school—the son of the head coach of the university's basketball team, Frederick, now a junior—and I felt, given our race, that it was only natural that Frederick and I should go to prom together.

What I knew of Frederick fit the stereotypes I had of Black people. He was the son of a basketball coach and played basketball himself. He had the slangy language. He slouched his lanky body through the halls in a way that was different—which is ordinarily taboo in high school, but with Frederick was appealing, intriguing, as if he didn't give a shit about looking so different from every other boy in the school. From a distance, I admired his easy Blackness. Yet it set him apart, put him out of reach, even for me. In the face of prom looming, I felt an urgent need to try to cross that line.

It was hard to work up the nerve to call him. I had spoken to him maybe once or twice in passing. But the potential awkwardness of going to a fancy dance with someone I hardly knew seemed outweighed by the logic of going to prom with a fellow Black person. A Black date felt like the safest possible choice. If only I could make it happen.

The day after I learned of Rob's plan to ask me to prom, I was ready to do an end run around him by asking Frederick instead. That afternoon after school, I grabbed the phone book off the kitchen counter and brought it upstairs to my bedroom where I could have some privacy. I grabbed my red Trimline phone from my desk and plunked down on my bed with the phone book and the phone. I opened the white pages and thumbed through the Cs until I found Frederick's last name. The address listed was in my town; it had to be the right number.

I could hear my heart beating against my skull, and I began to sweat a little while I rehearsed my opening lines twenty or thirty times. I imagined Frederick on the other end of the line. Would he even know who I was when I said my name? Should I try to speak with a bit of edgy jargon to sound Black enough to him? Did I even know any edgy jargon?

No.

Finally, I pulled the red phone onto my lap, lifted the receiver from the cradle, listened for the dial tone, and dialed the number. It rang three times, then someone answered. "H'lo?" The voice sounded distant. Uninterested. Like the fact of the phone ringing in his house was an annoyance. It must be Frederick, I thought. I began talking. At first he had no idea who I was so we stammered through an awkward back-and-forth where I explained that I was Julie, a sophomore. I knew my "white" voice wasn't going to communicate my race so I said I was *the* sophomore at school. The Black girl. Now that I knew he knew who I was, I took a deep breath and cut to the chase.

"Hey, so prom's coming up and I figure it's only logical that we go together."
"Yeah? Yeah."
"So—?"
"Yeah, yeah, no that makes sense."
"Cool. We'll go to prom then."
"Yeah."
"Okay great. Thanks. Bye."

The deed was done. But instead of the relief I'd expected would flood me, my blood continued pounding in my head. I was mortified. I'd just asked a guy to the prom whom I didn't even know, all because we both had brown skin. Isn't *that* racism?

Am I prejudiced? Can Black people even be prejudiced? What the hell kind of person am I?

I was also a little scared. What would it be like to go to the prom with a guy who was for all intents and purposes a stranger to me? And on top of that, a Black guy. What would it be like?

By the next day I was feeling ashamed. I walked through the halls at school preoccupied with thoughts about what I'd done to Frederick. He probably didn't want to go to the prom with some girl he barely knew. He deserved better. So did Rob, the guy I feared was settling for me and was trying to avoid.

I called Frederick back that night and told him a small lie. I told him I'd *just* heard Rob had been planning to ask me and now I felt badly that I'd jumped the gun.

"So, I guess you and I shouldn't go," I stammered.
"Okay, cool."

I went to prom with Rob dressed in a white Victorian-style dress that suited my mother's sensibilities, with a neckline that rose to the bottom of my chin. Decades later I can see that Rob was brave, even transgressive of social norms in asking me to prom. Maybe even that I was a girl he actually just wanted to take to prom.

Frederick and I never spoke again. His family moved away at the end of that school year. Later I'd learn that his father, who'd been the first Black head coach of any major sport in the Big Ten, had died of cancer just months before my stupid stunt.

XVIII.

At the very end of sophomore year, I started dating Mark, a Mormon boy in my grade whom I'd been crushing on for a while. He was smart, athletic, and cute in a Tom Cruise in *Risky Business* kind of way, and his conservative ideals made for fiery debates between us. Turns out he'd wanted to ask me to the prom and was kicking himself that Rob got to me first. He never knew about the awkward dance I'd done with Frederick.

"But Mormons don't like Black people," my mother reminded me, harking back to the years the Mormon missionaries visited our door in Snedens Landing when I was seven. She said this repeatedly, even as my relationship with Mark unfolded into months and then years.

She wasn't exactly wrong.

The Mormons have an appalling history on race. For most of their history, they believed—in accordance with their primary text, the *Book of Mormon*—that God cursed a certain tribe of people with "a skin of blackness." Because of this "truth" from the church's founding, church policy historically forbade men of color from being priests. The policy was finally repealed in 1978 when their church leader—known as the Prophet—received a direct revelation from God that Black men could "hold the priesthood." The Mormons use this 1978 "revelation" as "proof" that church practices do not yield to sociopolitical pressure and change only in response to divine revelation. Which I translate as: Yeah, the country may have bought into equal rights for Blacks in the 1960s, but we Mormons take our cues from God, and God didn't think Black men were equal to white men until 1978.

I started dating Mark five years after God changed his mind about Black people.

That I could envelop myself in a boy whose church believed this about my people was the seed of self-loathing lurking inside me that I could feel but could not yet identify. I spent more time at Mark's house than he did at mine because his parents were kind to me whereas mine were cordial at best to him. When I got invited to church activities, my mother visibly bristled. "You'll convert to that church over my dead body."

XIX.

If I had told my parents about the prom debacle with Frederick, I feared they would have been:

1) sad that I thought Rob's invitation to prom was a sign of him settling;
2) dismayed that I didn't know the one and only Black boy at my school;
3) busy examining my actions and words to discern my motivations (they would have discovered a self-loathing writhing at the heart of it);
4) shown the hazy outline of my wariness toward Black people;
5) unable to ignore the evidence that their interracial child experiment was failing.

They would have wondered what they'd done, whether they could have done anything, whether at that point anything could be done by anyone at all.

But I never told them.

And if, even without this prom fiasco information, they were concerned that their mixed-race child was struggling psychologically, they would have been right.

XX.

In the grand scheme of human existence my father and mother were an improbable couple. Their interracial relationship began in 1962 in West Africa, on the red-brown clay soil of Ghana's capital city, Accra.

My father, George I. Lythcott, was born in 1918 in New York, New York. His father, George Sr., was a Black physician with a medical degree from Boston University who was descended from the Lythcotts of British Guiana. His mother, Evelyn (Wilson) Lythcott, was a descendant of South Carolinian slaves whose father, Joshua, was Postmaster General of Florence, appointed by successive presidents and confirmed by successive senates throughout the late 1800s and into the early 1900s. Evelyn died from tuberculosis in 1920 in Florence. Daddy was not yet two.

Grandfather asked Evelyn's sister-in-law Lillian to look after Daddy until he could pull his life together and figure out a more long-term solution for Daddy's care. Walking up Lillian's pathway to visit his little boy one day, Grandfather could hear Lillian through the screen door shouting at Daddy. "Get your little Black hands off that chair." Evelyn's people were light; Lillian was considered "high yeller." Grandfather urgently sent for his sister Agatha in British Guiana and asked her to move to New York to care for Daddy there.

In 1925 Grandfather got married again to a woman named Corinne— half Black, half Cherokee freedman—and Daddy went to live with Grandfather and Corinne in Tulsa, Oklahoma. Daddy was now eight. Grandfather served the medical needs of Tulsa's Black community, some of whom could pay him with little more than livestock and produce. Corinne doted on Daddy as if he were her own son. She was the only mother he really ever knew.

Daddy came of age in the deeply segregated South. The thriving Black business community in Tulsa's Greenwood neighborhood, known as "the Black Wall Street," had been torched to the ground in 1921 by whites. Hundreds of Blacks were killed in the uprising, most of them lynched, and upward of ten thousand Black residents were left homeless when the damage was tallied. The massacre was labeled a "riot" and a few hundred Blacks were arrested. The lie was perpetuated for decades. In 1996, the Oklahoma state legislature would finally acknowledge that the prosperous Greenwood community had been set upon by white supremacists.

When Daddy was about sixteen, a little girl and her mother were walking along the road just beyond the house, and Daddy's dog, a large Doberman pinscher, got out of the yard, charged over to the young girl, and sank his teeth into her upper thigh. Daddy was terrified—it was his job to make sure the dog was chained up at all times—and he raced first to pull the dog off of the girl and then to get the girl to his father. Grandfather dressed the young girl's wound and then put the girl and her mother in his car to drive them home. The mother described where she lived in a vague manner, and Grandfather at first couldn't make sense of it. He soon realized that the family lived in a makeshift home at the edge of the town dump. He knew it was medically unsafe to send a child with such a bad wound back to that kind of home, but he didn't want to insult the woman, so he simply offered that the girl, Polly, might heal more quickly if he could clean and dress the wound each day, and perhaps she should live back at home with him, his wife Corinne, and Daddy, until the wound healed. The mother agreed. When the wound healed, the mother and Grandfather had a serious conversation about the girl's future. Grandfather officially adopted the little girl, who became my Aunt Polly.

After graduating from high school in Tulsa in 1935, Daddy went way up North to attend Bates College in Lewiston, Maine, where, as he would retell it to me with a chuckle decades later, there was only one Black man in each class, and one Black woman too, so the men would have someone to date.

Daddy ran track for Bates and was dubbed "the Oklahoma Flyer" by the student newspaper for consistently whizzing by his competitors with his lean, six-foot-two frame. In the spring of his freshman year, 1936, he qualified for the U.S. Olympic Trials. Another qualifier, the miler Jesse Owens, would go on to make the U.S. team and to stun Hitler with both his athletic prowess and his Blackness at the summer games in Berlin. Daddy helped pace Owens as he warmed up for his trial—a practice where four of the fastest quarter milers ran just ahead of Owens for one lap each so as to push Owens to run faster. But when it came time to compete in his own right, Daddy pulled his hamstring and had to abandon his Olympic dreams.

Daddy kept running for Bates in his remaining years at college as he pursued premedical studies; he was also quite involved in campus shenanigans. One night he pulled a cart full of hay up the hill above the football stadium, then set it on fire and gave it a push so it would roll back down the hill directly into the wooden stadium, which was quickly set ablaze. (No one complained; they'd been trying to garner support for a new stadium and now they *had* to build one.)

Another night, he coaxed a horse through the front door of the main administration building and led it up the steps leading to the offices on the second floor. He walked the horse into the president's office, scattered some hay on the floor, and shut the door. Then he crept down the stairs and out of the building, and went back to his dorm room. As any Oklahoma cowboy knows, horses will go up a set of stairs but will not come down. So the next morning when a secretary discovered the horse munching hay in the president's office as it gazed out through the big plate glass window overlooking the college green, the task of getting the horse down would be far more complicated than was the task of bringing him up. They had to hire a glazier to remove the large glass window and then bring in a crane to lift the horse down. Again, no one in the administration ever knew Daddy had done it.

Being one of a handful of Blacks at Bates grated on my father, but so did the stark class differences between himself and many of his peers; he was the son of a physician, yes, but a Black physician serving the Black community wasn't getting rich. Daddy resented the rich kids at Bates who had bicycles enabling them to get around campus and into town rather easily. One winter night Daddy stole a bunch of rich kids' bikes from around campus and threw them into the mountainous banks of snow that blanketed Lewiston each year. When the snow thawed the following spring, bikes kept emerging, rusty and bent, like muddy puddles, on the new, wet, green lawns.

Daddy was an anarchist, some might say. A prankster. A subversive. A rule-breaker. Some would say a thug. I see him as a Black man who in the construct of New England in the 1930s had little agency. He was a man of great intellect, tall and strong, still subject to being called "Boy" by any white man at any moment. He was capable and accomplished, yet subject to being second-guessed or blamed without cause. The pranks were perhaps his most vivid way of retaliation, of pulling the wool over their eyes. I imagine he felt a kind of raucous joy in accomplishing these subversive acts. *You think I'm bad? You have no idea how bad I am.* Yet each prank was just a brief burst of freedom from a cage. To our family's knowledge no one ever knew my father was behind any of these pranks. Or maybe they knew but didn't want to jeopardize the athletic eligibility of their track star and the recognition Bates College received whenever he ran.

Grandfather expected Daddy to follow in his footsteps and become a physician, but by junior year Daddy had taken a few courses in architecture, political science, and law. The possibility of law school began to tug on his attention. On April 29, 1938, Daddy's twentieth birthday, he sat down at the desk in his dorm room to tackle the difficult task of composing a letter to his father seeking formal permission to study law instead of medicine. He was still working on that letter into the night when his buddies came by to take him out to celebrate his birthday. Daddy and his friends went out and had a good time, and he got back to the dormitory quite late that night. The next morning he awoke to a telegram telling him to come home because his father was dying. Daddy took the first available train and made the long trek from Maine to Oklahoma, but when he arrived on May 1, his father was already gone. Never having gained his father's permission to pursue law, Daddy pursued medicine.

Like his father, Daddy graduated from the medical school at Boston University (1943) and his expertise in pediatrics kept him first in the Boston area, where he and his new wife, Ruth, settled for a time and where their four children were born in 1945, 1946, 1948, and 1950. Ruth began to suffer from mental illness, which grew steadily worse. In 1953 Daddy was called up for military service at Mitchel Air Force Base on Long Island, and after that he set up a private pediatric practice in New York where he treated the children of prominent Blacks, including Jackie Robinson, Nat King Cole, and Harry Belafonte. Because their mother was by this time quite ill, the children went to live in Tulsa with Daddy's stepmother, Corinne.

In 1956 Daddy and Ruth moved to Oklahoma, where Daddy took a position at the medical school at the University of Oklahoma in Oklahoma City. The *Pittsburgh Courier* reported on November 3, 1956, "For the first time in the history of the institution a Negro has been appointed to the faculty of the University of Oklahoma." It went on, "a specialist in the diseases of infants and children, [Lythcott] was recently appointed clinical assistant in pediatrics in the university's School of Medicine, and became the first and only Negro holding such a position in a Southern university." He received an NIH grant to establish the nation's first well-baby clinic on an Indian reservation nearby. While serving on the faculty Daddy also maintained a private pediatrics practice for Black patients, and, like his father before him, was often paid with things like produce and desserts.

Daddy's children, my half siblings, Ruth, George, Michael, and Stephen, were raised in the Jim Crow South. The civil rights movement began to emerge around them, and in the early years the movement was populated heavily by young people. My sister Ruth, the eldest of Daddy's children, was twelve when she first participated in events organized by the NAACP Youth Council. She was fourteen in 1959 when she decided to participate in sit-ins at a lunch counter at a downtown restaurant. She took our brothers, then ages twelve, eleven, and nine, with her. Daddy knew this was happening and allowed it. One day, the television was on in his office and he saw police dragging Ruthie and Stevie out of a building.

In the early 1960s Oklahoma's School of Medicine was searching for a new dean. The committee mentioned the fact of Daddy to the finalist, who said it would be no problem. But when the finalist became dean, he didn't speak to Daddy for a year. Finally, he summoned Daddy to his office and issued a warning. "I can't have someone on my faculty I can't invite over to my house for dinner." Daddy was being told to quit.

When, in 1962, the U.S. government asked Daddy to join a team headed to Ghana in West Africa to help the Ghanaians establish an organization akin to the National Institutes of Health here in the U.S., he jumped at the opportunity. He'd be Deputy Director of a large team and would focus his own research on a measles vaccine, which would be an important step in his career.

But what of his children? Daddy and Ruth were now separated and she was not well enough to care for the children. Corinne was elderly and growing frail, and couldn't consider making such a huge relocation herself. Men rarely played the role of single parent in those times. A colleague advised Daddy to farm out his kids—now sixteen, fifteen, fourteen, and twelve—to four different families. But breaking the family into bits was an untenable choice for Daddy. Deep down he was convinced that he could handle the challenge. Hell, he was going off to Africa . . . raising four kids there was doable, *had to be doable*. He needed to get not just himself but his four children out of the increasingly volatile American South.

Officially a U.S. diplomat, Daddy shipped himself, the kids, their station wagon, and much of their belongings over six thousand miles to West Africa, and moved them into their new home in Ghana's capital city, Accra, in a section of town called Korle-Bu.

For the first time in Daddy's life, skin color wasn't the primary mechanism for evaluating the worth of a human, not the determining factor for whether he'd be allowed or rejected as he tried to make his way in the world. Dark though he was, he was to some Ghanaians "Obruni"—a term in the Twi language for someone not from Africa, a term used, even, for whites. But being Obruni didn't constrain Daddy's options. He felt a psychological freedom unavailable to him in America—and finally began to emerge into himself as a man. This was the state of things when he went to a party one night in Korle-Bu and met Jeannie, the woman who would become my mother.

A few months before Daddy graduated from Bates College in 1939, my mother, Jean Snookes, was born to a white working-class family in Yorkshire, England. Her grandfathers had worked in the coal mines, and her father, a schoolteacher, served in World War II, fighting in the Battle of Britain, leaving behind three very young children—my mother, her older brother, and her younger brother—and a wife barely able to make ends meet with the rations that came from the British government. Mom recalls the air-raid sirens blaring night after night as the Germans tried to locate and bomb Yorkshire's coal mines and steel production facilities, and the nightly ritual of battening the hatches to remove any trace of light from the night sky to conceal themselves from the German pilots. The Britons defeated Hitler so conclusively in the Battle of Britain that Hitler turned his focus elsewhere. Winston Churchill declared, "Never in human history have so many owed so much to so few." When the war finally ended and her father came home, Mom was six years old.

Her family continued to struggle financially. After the war her parents had two more children and when her mother procured a treat for them—such as an apple—they would split it five ways. My mother was a gifted learner who worked tirelessly and was always one of the strongest students in her school, especially in science and math courses, and she rose to the rank of "Head Girl" based on her academic performance. She was the first in her family to go to university and attended the University of Manchester, where she studied honors science. There, she met and fell in love with a young man named Ian Forrester, an Honors Math student who was on the gymnastics team and rode a motorcycle.

In late 1958 Mom was about to turn twenty and was four months pregnant with Ian's child. They were due to be married in a few weeks when Ian fell ill suddenly with severe abdominal pain. The doctor at the University Health Center said liver trouble was going around the university. The pain would be severe but it would soon abate. Take some pills, come back Monday. The doctor had failed to properly diagnose the source of Ian's pain: an adhesion of the appendix.

Mom stayed by Ian's bedside for four days trying to nurse him through this awful pain, but she grew extremely worried—he seemed so very sick. She called upon Ian's landlord, who agreed something was terribly wrong and drove the two of them to Ian's parents' home in the town of Hanley. Although Ian had told them about her and about the baby, this was to be Mom's first time meeting Ian's family.

Ian's parents went to their family doctor and he came back to the house with them. Looking at Ian, the doctor seemed to Mom to be dubious about the university physician's diagnosis, but it being the university physician, the family doctor didn't want to second-guess the situation. He said he would come back the following morning but stressed to Ian's parents that they should come get him if Ian's condition changed at all. (Ian's parents had no phone.)

Ian's condition did change—the terrible pain went away later that day—which his parents took as a good sign. Ian asked his parents if Mom could come up to his bedroom to see him, which caused some consternation since she and Ian were unmarried. But these circumstances threw regular rules into relief and his parents agreed. Mom entered Ian's bedroom and saw his belly blown up like a huge balloon. His skin was an awful gray color. He looked like a shadow of himself, she told me.

The family doctor came as promised early the next morning, took one look at Ian, and raced out the door to call for an ambulance. Doctors operated immediately. Hours later Ian's father took Mom to see him in recovery. She wanted to crawl up into the bed with him, but the sides were pulled up high on his hospital bed to prevent his attempts at escape. She could only stand on her tiptoes to lean over the barrier and kiss him. As she did so, Ian spoke.

"Marry me, kid," he pleaded, using his pet name for her.
"Just as soon as you get out of here, Love, we will do it."

Mom realized only later that Ian had known he was dying, had known he needed to spare her the stigma of being an unwed mother, had needed to marry her right then and there.

She went back to the house with Ian's father. Later that night there was a knock at the door. It was a local policeman relaying a message from the hospital that they must come quickly because Ian was dying. But Mom did not know about the knock at the door or the message, would not know this until the night's events were relayed to her the following day. Ian's parents decided that in her "condition" Mom would not be able to handle what would come next.

Ian's father had gone to the hospital alone that night while Ian's mother stayed home with her three younger children and Mom. He arrived just as a priest emerged from Ian's room. He'd been administering last rites and now looked around and asked, "Who is Jean?" The doctor told Ian's father he could have saved Ian if he'd had him twenty-four hours sooner. When Mom learned this she was shattered. She would blame herself for these elapsed hours for the rest of her life.

In May 1959 Mom gave birth to their baby, whom she named Ian after his father. Her parents bucked the tide of decency and reputation extant at the time by allowing Mom and Little Ian to come live with them and by being emotionally supportive. Big Ian's parents were supportive too—agreeing that the baby would have their last name even though Mom and Ian had not been married. Mom graduated from university the following year with honors, and with her dean's support applied for and received a full scholarship to do a PhD in Saskatoon, Saskatchewan, Canada. The scholarship would pay for everything once she got herself and Little Ian to Canada; the stumbling block was how to find the money to travel there. She went for a loan at her bank but had only her trustworthiness as collateral, which was not enough.

She applied for a few teaching jobs locally but the fact of Little Ian (and his status as a "bastard," which was the prevailing ideology at the time) was a stigma not to be overcome. Finally, after her father pulled some strings in the district in which he'd worked for over ten years, she got a teaching position in Sheffield, found day care for Little Ian, and moved there. The school's headmaster said, "No one is to know about the baby," except, the headmaster said, for his deputy Mr. Braxton, who the headmaster felt needed to know. Mom worked at the Sheffield school for two years. Braxton began to blackmail Mom, forcing her into an unwanted sexual relationship with him in order to keep the news of Little Ian quiet. Little Ian came down with double pneumonia—pneumonia in both lungs—and almost died.

Mom was beginning to give up. She blamed herself for Little Ian's poor health and for not getting Big Ian to the hospital sooner. Braxton demanded to know her whereabouts at all times, who she was with, and what she was up to. She had few prospects for a better life in England and began applying for various teaching fellowships in other countries again, desperate for a better outcome this time.

In 1962, when he was not yet three, Mom gave Little Ian up for adoption to Big Ian's parents, via a formal proceeding. She and Little Ian would not reunite until 1977, when he was eighteen and she was legally allowed to contact him. I was ten. I recall my mother taking me on a walk in our Madison neighborhood to tell me that I had another sibling, in England, and I recall feeling angry to have been kept in the dark on something so important. She quickly set me straight. "How does a mother tell one child she has given up another?" she said. "I needed you to be old enough not to worry whether I might give you up, too." I stared off in the distance blinking away tears.

Shortly after giving Little Ian up for adoption, Mom left England, having accepted a teaching fellowship at Ghana's Pre-Nursing Training School— the first fellowship offered that would pay her airfare to the country on top of providing her a house to live in. She boarded an airplane for the first time in her life for a flight that took her from London thirty-one hundred and fifty-nine miles due south down the Greenwich meridian. She landed in Accra, where she was met by a new colleague, who drove her to her new home at Number Four Nimtree Circle in Korle-Bu. The colleague brought her small suitcase from the trunk, then pulled away as she stood looking up at her new home, a second-floor walk-up over the garage with a circular staircase to one side. There'd be no need for that garage; she didn't know how to drive and was, as she called it, "poor as a church mouse." She was twenty-three.

One evening soon after Mom arrived in the country, the head of the Pre-Nursing Training School had her over for dinner to introduce her to a few more people in the community. At about ten p.m. she was walking the short distance home along the dusty red-brown road when a car pulled alongside her. It was Fran, a nurse on the American medical team in Korle-Bu. Fran had spotted Mom three or four times before on her walk to or from work and had given her a ride, and the two of them had started to become friendly. Fran leaned out of her car window.

"It's too late for you to be walking alone. Let me give you a ride."

Mom got in the car. As Mom's house came into view, Fran slowed down and nodded back toward the trunk of the car. "Actually, we're having a party and I left to go get more beer. I'm headed back there now. You should come."

Mom looked over at her house. A party with the Americans probably required a fancier outfit than she'd worn to the dinner. She had one elegant dress to her name and it was in a closet in her bedroom at the top of those stairs.

She shook her head, said she'd need to change first. But Fran was in a hurry to get back to the party.

"You look fine. C'mon."

Mom gave in. Fran turned the car around and a few minutes later they arrived at the party now in full swing.

Mom was curious about people and gregarious, so she quickly found herself in conversation with other partygoers. A short while later Daddy arrived, making a stir in the crowd because of his high status in the diplomat community and because he had on his arm the sister of the American writer James Baldwin. Baldwin was on an official visit to Accra, and the embassy had tasked Daddy with taking his sister out for the evening before her midnight Pan Am flight back to the States.

Mom and Daddy soon found themselves on the same side of the living room and struck up a conversation. Forty-five minutes later Daddy looked at his watch and realized he had to get Baldwin's sister to the airport. It was eleven fifteen p.m. He asked Mom if she would wait.

"I can't promise. I'm here with Fran. I have to leave when Fran does."
"Well, if you're not here when I get back, can I come see you tomorrow then?"
She didn't hesitate. "Yes."

Daddy left. A short while later Fran was ready to go. When Daddy returned to the party sometime later, Mom was gone.

The next day—a Saturday, Mom rose early. She didn't know when Daddy was coming by and she wanted to be ready. She bathed, put on the special dress she'd wanted to be in the night before, made up her face, dabbed herself with perfume, and fluffed her hair just so. She walked over to the window that faced the road and peeked through the blinds. She could see much of the neighborhood from the second story and saw no sign of Daddy. But it was early—only nine a.m.

Accra is four degrees north of the equator so even the smallest movements can cause a person to sweat, particularly a person unaccustomed to the heat, as Mom was in her first months in Ghana. So she felt it was best to sit as still as possible on the couch and wait for Daddy. She finished a book she'd been reading. Then she began working a crossword in one of the many puzzle and logic books she'd brought with her from England. She got up to stretch her legs and stirred the heavy heat with her movements. The click of her heels on the floor disturbed the silence. She sat down and did more puzzles. Got up to make a sandwich. More puzzles. Hours went by and still she waited, trying to keep cool. Finally, at six p.m., as the sun made its quick drop to the horizon, she gave herself a stern talking-to. *What makes you think a man like him—a doctor— would be interested in you?*

She woke the next day feeling frustrated, not just over her foolishness in thinking this man might actually want to see her again, but because in spending an entire day waiting for him she'd neglected her housework. She put on a pair of old shorts and a T-shirt and began by making her bed, cleaning the bathroom, and putting dishes away. Then she settled in for a morning of furniture polishing. At about noon she heard the scrunch of tires on her gravel driveway and peeked out the window. It was a huge Mercury station wagon with wings at the back. "It was him, at my house," she'd tell me years later. "I was mortified to be in grubby shorts polishing furniture but here he was. That's the thought that took over. That's what mattered."

Daddy pulled his car to a stop in front of the tree at the end of Mom's driveway. Took the circular stairway two steps at a time and knocked on her door. She welcomed him in and they sat on her couch and talked for hours. Then, just as before, he looked at his watch and knew he had to leave. This time he needed to be home with his four kids. They parted. But they were together from that hot Sunday afternoon in Accra until his death on a Saturday thirty-three years later off the coast of Massachusetts on the island of Martha's Vineyard. My unlikely parents.

Mom soon met Daddy's children—Ruth, George, Michael, and Stephen, who, at sixteen, fifteen, fourteen, and twelve years old, were much closer in age to her than she was to their father. They attended a local boarding school and when Daddy traveled back to the States for six weeks, Mom brought the children the things they needed at school and handled his affairs as a secretary might or perhaps even a wife. Over the ensuing months their attitudes toward her ranged from bemused, to indifferent, to warm, to skeptical, to defiant, and even, at times, to hostile. A year later, Mom was writing regular letters to Daddy's stepmother, Corinne, back in Oklahoma to update her on the family's goings-on. Like Daddy's children, Corinne experienced her own range of emotions about this white woman Daddy was dating who was now writing to her. But on one of Daddy's many trips back to the States, Corinne gave him her ring for when it came time to propose.

He did propose, on a sandy beach along the road to the fishing village of Tema, which President Kwame Nkrumah correctly envisioned would be an international seaport one day. They married in January of 1966 in Accra in a civil ceremony, with only three witnesses, a white man and two white women. The clerk initially mistook the white man to be my mother's intended husband. Then the huge ceiling fan doing its best to keep the air a few degrees above stifling ruffled the pages of the clerk's text and he began reading the procedures for divorce. But they sorted it all out with a chuckle and managed to get married in a ceremony that would have been illegal in seventeen states back in the U.S. at the time.

They moved to Lagos, Nigeria, later that year, when my father joined the historic effort to try to eradicate smallpox and was put in charge of the operation in twenty West African countries. One by one first Ruth and then George had left for college in the States, and then Michael left as well. I was born at the tail end of this adventure, in November 1967, at Lagos Teaching Hospital. Stephen was the only sibling still in Africa when I was born, and he brought me a dark purple fuzzy stuffed animal with long hair. Ruth sent me a Black baby doll. I'd keep both of these toys for years. The West African smallpox effort succeeded a year and a half ahead of schedule and the disease was declared eradicated from the globe in 1980.

When I was four weeks old we headed back to Accra to spend Christmas with my parents' friend, the American Ambassador to Ghana, Franklin Williams, and his wife. Daddy's driver, a Nigerian man named Eric, sped us across the coastal road from Lagos through Dahomey (now Benin), through Togo, and into Ghana, a trek of over three hundred miles. While we were there, a political skirmish broke out in Nigeria related to the Biafran civil war; there were new contentions that children were starving in the Biafra region, and the U.S. government asked Daddy to return to Nigeria immediately to assess the situation. We would have to fly. Daddy hastily drew up the papers Eric would need by way of explanation for himself as he drove alone through the borders of Ghana, Togo, Dahomey, back to Nigeria. Eric dropped us off at the Accra airport. Mom held me in her arms as she and Daddy went through immigration.

"Where's her passport?" spurted the immigration officer, nodding in my direction.

"She's only four weeks old," Daddy stated, with the authority of a pediatrician and the airs of a diplomat.

"She's a person, isn't she?"

As would be the case often in Daddy's life, his rhetoric and authoritative manner would win the day. Though I lacked any identifying evidence of my existence or citizenship, I was permitted to exit Ghana and, a short plane flight later, permitted to enter Nigeria.

America recognized citizenship through either parent, although Britain only recognized it through the father, so British citizenship was never an option for me. Nigeria's rule was that I could claim citizenship up until I was eighteen if I wanted to do so. I never did and really can't say why. Nor did my parents. Indifference? An unwillingness to confront the red tape in a foreign country? A sense that I would never "need" it? A few months after the tense moments at the airport in Accra, I would have my own passport certifying me as American—the only citizenship I've ever had. My parents never dreamed that the American-ness of my citizenship—and that of countless others born to an American outside the U.S.—would ever be the subject of political debate. To them, my being of mixed race might be a contentious issue in my life, but when it came to citizenship, they foresaw no question. I was an American.

XXI.

My American passport took me many places over the years—to visit my British relatives, to a family vacation in Jamaica, and to France when I was fifteen.

The France trip was the summer after my sophomore year of high school, a few months after I'd tried to avoid going to the prom with Rob by inviting Frederick. It was a three-week exchange trip organized by the daughter-in-law of my Auntie Polly (my father's adopted sister). Aunt Polly's daughter-in-law, who taught French at an elite New England prep school, had invited me to join her class since I, too, was studying French in high school. Though the kids were all white, and all affluent, I quickly found a connection with them because they were worldly, familiar with places beyond their hometowns, unlike most of the kids with whom I was attending high school. Some of the kids listened to music on their Sony Walkmans. The Police's new album, *Synchronicity*, was a huge hit among these kids and allowed them to tune out during our long plane flight to Paris.

We traveled on the red-eye and emerged bleary-eyed into Charles de Gaulle Airport. We then boarded the Paris Métro, which would take us to our youth hostel. The train was packed when we got on and we had to stand in the center, hanging on to the shiny metal poles for balance as the train bumped along the tracks beneath the city. I gripped my purse, my hand on the zipper. The crowd got thicker with every stop and at one point I was jostled by what looked like a tribe of small, ragged children. Moments later, I realized my purse was unzipped and my wallet was gone. My Aunt Polly's daughter-in-law took me to the police station while the rest of our group settled in at the youth hostel. It's not like I'd lost much. I was fifteen. All I had in there were a handful of traveler's checks and a photo of my boyfriend, Mark. But I felt ashamed. I'd been assaulted by, of all people, small white children.

A few days later I stayed behind after our language lesson at a local university to ask the professor a question and then found myself walking back to our youth hostel alone. I came upon a small park where a little white girl of no more than ten was kicking the gravel out of her shoes. As I neared, she stopped what she was doing, looked up at me, and spoke.

"Pourquoi es-tu noire?" (Why are you Black?)

Decades later I would read the work of Frantz Fanon, who had also had a humiliating encounter with a little white French girl. But on that day as a fifteen-year-old walking through Paris I was alone with just my rudimentary French and my fragile sense of self.

"Pourquoi es-tu noire?" she demanded.
"Parce que j'ai de la chance." (Because I am lucky.)

I didn't believe it. But I wanted to. I hoped my words would send this little stranger home with some big questions. Maybe they'd even fuck her up a little bit. I didn't mind. As far as I was concerned, she was every white person who had ever questioned my right to exist, to be a regular person just going through my day without drawing the scrutiny or fascination of others. I didn't want to make excuses or give this little girl a lesson in anthropology. I wanted to fucking shine. I wanted to shine so fucking much that that little white French girl would ache to be me. Ache like me.

XXII.

While I was in France a new family moved into the vacant house next door. Soon after I got home I met their eldest daughter, Stacey, a girl my age who hit me smooth, sweet, and strong, like a shot of single malt scotch.

Stacey was from Alabama. She was white, but she knew Black people. As she told me stories from her childhood in the South, I secretly interrogated her words for every clue, studying what she knew to learn more about my own kind.

She had a stash of Prince's cassette tapes her parents forbade her to listen to. One tape was actually contraband—illegal for distribution in America—but Stacey was the kind of girl who could get her hands on such things. Sitting in my car with Stacey we listened to "Little Red Corvette," "Soft and Wet," "Bambi," "I Wanna Be Your Lover," and my favorite, "Controversy."

Stacey and I pierced our ears in her upstairs bathroom with some blocks of ice and a safety pin. She was my first transgressive friend, transgressing her parents' rules, transgressing rules for girls, transgressing whiteness. She crossed all kinds of borders into the liminal space, which is where she found me—floundering about like I was learning to swim and looking for something stable to hold on to.

XXIII.

By the time junior year began Frederick's family had moved away, making me officially the only Black kid in the twelve-hundred-member student body at Middleton High School. I knew to banter with the boys who mocked my hair and I shrugged off the observations about how un-Black my voice sounded. I worked my way to the top of the school's various ranks:

1. Doing very well in school, I was one of the kids our chemistry teacher teased for being "college-bound."
2. I had a boyfriend.
3. I was on the Pompon team.
4. I was vice president of my class. (My boyfriend Mark was president for the second year in a row, and I couldn't bring myself to run against him.)

This was my normal. If it was a balancing act, you'd barely have seen a wobble. I was coping without knowing I was coping. Like wearing a shirt inside out all day long without ever realizing it.

XXIV.

In the spring of my junior year, 1984, I was sixteen and the Reverend Jesse Jackson was making a serious run for the Democratic nomination for President of the United States. My parents were staunchly liberal and Democrats, and one night at dinner my mom started talking about Jesse Jackson and the headway he was making vis-à-vis the other Democratic candidates. Daddy shook his head. "It'll never happen." He wasn't interested in the oughts and shoulds or even the coulds; he was a realist. Listening to Mom, though, I began to feel a stirring in myself, a lightness from just contemplating the possibility of a big weight being lifted off my shoulders. *Our* shoulders. Doing the dishes that night, I found myself thinking about whether a Black man being taken seriously as a candidate for President might somehow lift this cloak of presumed inadequacy off of us all.

A few weeks later, when my English teacher asked us to write a persuasive essay, I chose to write about the Jackson campaign. None of my liberal friends thought he should win. None of them thought he *could* win. I didn't know enough about the various policy points to make a strong case for which candidate was most qualified to lead our nation. Instead, I wrote my paper about the symbolic significance of Jackson's campaign—that it was profoundly powerful for Black people to see a Black person run; that it was making us feel more equal. More human. More American.

When it was my turn to present my paper, I got up out of my desk, walked to the front of the class, and turned around to face my classmates, anticipating the power of the words I had written and my ability to deliver them well with my reading. Oratory, I knew from having given more than my share of speeches as a student leader, was a strength of mine. When I was done presenting, though, there was just silence, and in the silence I heard that neither my classmates nor my English teacher were terribly persuaded by what I'd had to say. In fact, my teacher felt I was so off the mark that he required me to rewrite the essay. When I stood before my classmates for a second time, it was evident from their faux-confused question-asking that maybe I was the one who was confused for thinking that the fact of Jesse Jackson's candidacy meant anything. To anyone. Who mattered.

XXV.

That same year the College Board awarded me a National Merit Commendation for being an "Outstanding Negro Student." In theory it was an honor. But it felt like an insult twice over: my own little Pyrrhic victory.

It was 1984 for Christ's sake. "Negro" was derogatory in our nation's racial lexicon—one step above "Colored," which was one step above the dreaded N-word. We were now Black. Even Afro American. How could the College Board not know this?

And I hardly deserved an award tied to race. A few of my friends were among the "real" National Merit scholars at our school, so this was stark evidence that I hadn't done as well as them on the PSAT; I was just at the top of the heap of Black folks, which was a heap we all knew I didn't belong to.

When a hired photographer came to shoot sports and clubs photos for our school yearbook, all us National Merit people were given a time to pose for photos as well. The other students goofed around in mock self-deprecation over their achievement and I stood off to the side of the group acting as if I hadn't really been invited. The photographer yelled at the rest of them to stand still and pose. Then, with my classmates finally assembled in two lines, the photographer pointed at me.

"You. Are you in this too?"

I swallowed hard and strode over to my classmates, and offered in a jaunty tone: "Here comes the Negro." Then I took my place on my tiptoes behind the second row.

I desperately did not want this attention, this so-called recognition for being a great "Negro" in the eyes of the organization that was every student's gateway to college. I also felt like an impostor for getting an award that should go to a *real* Black kid, some kid somewhere else who most certainly deserved the recognition more than I did.

XXVI.

We are a college-educated family; when it came time for me to think about applying, it was a question not of whether to go to college but where.

During spring break of my junior year, Mom and I took a road trip out of Wisconsin to the East Coast to visit a dozen or so schools in the span of ten days. After eight hours of driving Interstate 80 east through Illinois, Indiana, and into Ohio, we were ready to pull over for the night, only to learn there were no vacancies—none for one hundred miles due to a big convention, we were told. We pulled into a McDonald's parking lot outside of Cleveland, reclined our seats, locked the car doors, and slept in the car. The next morning, we went back into McDonald's to brush our teeth and wash our faces. There was little I could do in those circumstances with my hair.

By the following night we'd made it all the way to Hanover, New Hampshire, where we stayed in a motel. The next morning, we showered and I put on a pretty drop-waist dress that was lilac with little white flecks, and we headed off for our tour at Dartmouth College. Our tour began in the library, which was full of students at long tables and computer terminals, and I edged my way toward the front of the group so as to talk with the student guide while Mom hung back with the other parents. As we were headed out of the library there was some kind of commotion behind me, and I glanced back to see a Black boy who had leaned too far back in his chair at a computer terminal and was flailing to right himself.

Later, my mom told me that when I'd walked past that boy, she'd seen him do a double take and continue to follow me with his eyes to the point where he'd had to lean way, way back on two legs of his chair. Between the lines of Mom's story I could read her dreams for me: There are Black people out there. Not only that. Maybe Black friends. Maybe even a Black boy who would find me beautiful.

As she spoke I tried to act cool. But I could feel my heartbeat pounding in my veins. We drove from Hanover to Boston, to New York, and to Pennsylvania, visiting school after school after school, and I replayed my mother's story again and again in my head and interlaced it with the image I still had of that boy in my mind. Maybe there'd be boys like him at these colleges. Maybe I'd feel more normal once I got out of Middleton High. In the privacy of my own mind, I blushed.

XXVII.

At the start of my senior year, I was serving my class as vice president for the third year in a row and was also elected president of the student council. *The Cosby Show* debuted on NBC in September. With the show's father, Cliff Huxtable, being a doctor like Daddy, and the middle daughter, Denise, looking kind of like me, there was finally a fictional family on the TV screen that resembled mine. I was glued to it every Thursday evening, reading it for guidance about how to be someone like me.

I turned seventeen that November, a few weeks after the presidential election that reelected Ronald Reagan. My best friend, Diana, made me a huge birthday locker sign filled with words and images cut from the pages of *Tiger Beat*, *Seventeen*, and other teen magazines. She'd woken up extra early to get to school in time to tape it to my locker before my arrival. We did this kind of thing for each other. Her birthday was earlier in November and I'd festooned her locker just two weeks before.

Something about turning seventeen made me want to look like the woman I was becoming. Getting ready for school that morning, I'd pulled the curling iron through my hair over and over again, and smoothed it into a nice, sleek, low ponytail that would hang from the nape of my neck. I'd spent a few extra moments on my makeup, carefully drawing the charcoal eyeliner across my lids, swishing the black mascara along my lashes, contouring my cheeks with chestnut blush, and painting my lips raisin. I'd selected a beautiful black wool dress to wear, a professional cut with long sleeves, a round neck, and the shoulder pads that were the fashion at the time. I'd pulled nylons over my strong calves and thighs, and, to finish the look, I wore a pair of black patent leather pumps that made me three inches taller. Decades later I would read a short story by Julie Orringer that described a middle-aged woman as "no longer ripening but not yet deteriorating." Back at my house in Cherrywood on that November morning, I was ripening. Beautifully. And I knew it.

I drove the snowy route to school, pulled my car into a spot in the far parking lot, got out, and walked on tiptoe toward the main building, deftly avoiding the permanent fixtures of ice and lumps of hard snow that clumped on the asphalt in wintertime in Wisconsin. As I walked up to the main entrance of the school, I saw my reflection in the glass doors, my dark figure silhouetted against the bright white snow behind me.

I entered the school and headed left toward my locker, which was located in the bank reserved for seniors in the central hallway near the administration's offices, conveniently close to everything. Even above the din of student voices and slamming lockers, I could hear my heels clicking with precision on the shiny cement floor.

I could already see the birthday locker sign fifty lockers in front of me, with its five sheets of white paper taped one to the next to the next in a sort of vertical column with shimmering silver ribbons taped to the top and sides spiraling out into the hall. I felt a surge of anticipation of the attention I would get that day. A friend shouted "Happy Birthday" as I made my way down the hall, and I nodded, smiled, and shouted, "Thanks!"

When I got to my locker I stood and admired Diana's creativity, reading from top to bottom all the bits of language and imagery she'd gone to such trouble to cut out and glue on there for me. I opened the locker, put my backpack inside, and pulled out the books I needed for my first two classes. Then I turned and smiled at someone else saying "Happy Birthday," clanged the locker door shut, and twisted the combination lock a few times. I strode down the main corridor toward my first class feeling like I owned the place.

Some unknown minutes later, someone took a thick black marker and wrote "Niger" in three places on my birthday locker sign. Even spelled incorrectly, I knew what they'd meant. I spotted it in late morning during the passing time between classes and immediately my mouth went dry.

I stood with my back against my locker, affecting casual, as the other students opened and shut their locker doors. After an excruciatingly long three minutes of metal scraping on metal and the roar of chatter and movement, and a few more "Happy Birthday's," the hall began to empty as kids went off to their next class. The bell rang, signaling the start of class.

I walked quickly toward the school office, which sat at the crossroads of this hallway and the other main hall. The hallway ramped up just before the intersection, and at the top of it I paused, my chest heaving, my mouth still dry. I had to get my shit together. The glass-walled office was around the corner to the right. I took a deep breath, then drew my spine up straight, smoothed my ponytail, straightened my dress, plastered my most pleasing smile on my face, and strode with casual confidence over to the glass door of the main office and flung it wide open.

As President of the Student Council I knew all the secretaries. Marie sat at the main desk and didn't bat an eyelash over why I was not in class. I asked her if I could borrow a black Magic Marker. She fished around in her drawer. "Will this do?" I took the marker from her with a smile, thanked her, pushed the door open, and walked out of the office. At the intersection I scanned all directions, then turned left and walked quickly back to my locker. When I reached it, I looked down the long hallway once more to make sure no one was coming, and then, as the silence pressed down around me, I took the cap off the marker and began to draw neat black lines over each iteration of the word. I now had three black boxes where the words had been. I turned around and pressed my back into my locker, still clutching the marker, my knees sinking a little bit toward the floor.

At day's end I took the sign home. In the privacy of my bedroom I pulled my senior year scrapbook from the bookshelf above my desk and opened it to the first blank page. There, I pasted my birthday locker sign accordion style, so that it could be completely unfolded to resemble what it had looked like hanging on my locker. Before closing the scrapbook, I took a pair of scissors and, like a surgeon excising tumors, removed the three iterations of the shameful word, then threw them in the trash. I closed the scrapbook and returned it to the shelf containing the recorded history of my childhood.

XXVIII.

Over the Christmas holiday I typed my college applications on a brand-new Apple 2E computer my parents were among the first to buy. In March 1985 the first Internet domain name, "symbolics.com," was registered. In April, I accepted an offer of admission to Stanford University.

A classmate, Harris, had applied to Stanford but had not gotten in. Harris and I were in pre-calculus together (the highest math class at our school), and it was held during the seventh and final period of the day. One day in April, right after the bell rang signaling the end of class, Harris's father walked in, sat down at an empty desk next to mine, and began talking to me in a playful tone.

"*Sooo*, you got into Stanford?"

I looked up at my friend Harris and silently asked, *Why is your dad here?* Then I replied. "Yes."

"So, what were your SAT scores?"

I responded.

"Do you think it's fair that you got into Stanford over Harris when his scores were higher than that?"

Harris was not the president of the student council. Our grades were roughly the same. But I had stolen his spot at Stanford with my Blackness.

XXIX.

A Black male sophomore enrolled at Middleton High School that spring. I never met him. Late one day, word spread that the boy had been beaten up in a second-floor bathroom and the N-word was found scrawled on the tiled wall. A shudder ran through the school community—to have both a new Black male and violence against a Black male in our community felt fictional yet inevitable. It was as if the violence were playing out according to a trope, caused by the Black male's arrival or by something he had done consistent with stereotype, instead of racial hatred lurking beneath the surface eager to pounce. I had seen it pounce. It had pounced on me. But there had been no witnesses and I hadn't told.

I was in economics class when I heard the news, and a male friend of mine said he wanted to escort me to and from class and to and from my car. I don't think I've ever been offered a greater act of service in my life.

The school board convened a meeting to "think about these race issues" and invited Daddy to "help." My boyfriend Mark and I were also invited, in our capacity as student body leaders. Together, the three of us walked toward the district building. I could sense from the stiff strength of Daddy's stride and the impatient look on his face that he was frustrated. All of a sudden our Blackness was front and center. What's more, they *needed* us to be Black. To help them *do something*. I could tell that Mark was frustrated too—his lips were pursed in a thin line and his normally warm eyes were cold and distant. Later I'd ask him about it and he'd tell me he was frustrated that the conversation had to happen at all; that in contemplating imposing a hate speech code, the school was curtailing civil liberties.

I walked between the two men who mattered most to me and mulled frustrations of my own. Normally Mark and I would hold hands as we walked but I sensed that to do so in these circumstances was to take sides. And I was too old to hold Daddy's hand.

I walked, between the two men who mattered most to me, alone.

XXX.

Unlike in Reston where our Jack and Jill chapter was made up of families who lived within a five-mile radius, in South Central Wisconsin we had to draw a much bigger circle to find enough middle-class Black families to field a monthly meeting.

The absurdity of gathering up all the Black people in the middle of nowhere Wisconsin and trying to call it meaningful grated on my nerves. It was me the Black kid from Verona meeting up with some other Black kid who lived three towns over meeting up with the handful of kids who lived in Madison. Maybe there were seven of us. Somehow, our parents seemed to think, spending a few hours together every few months would—what? Help us find community? Help us be ourselves? One month the Greater Madison group (as we were known) met with the Milwaukee group, which had about twenty-five kids, and we all went to the mall together. What teenager wants to hang out with teenagers who know each other but don't know you? I trudged along from store to store, wishing the charade would end.

In spring of my senior year, the Milwaukee chapter hosted a cotillion. I'd never heard of such a thing so my mother explained: a cotillion was like a debutante ball (I didn't know what that was either) and this one would be a big fancy gathering of Black people with some kind of "coming-out" ceremony for the girls and formal dancing. She spoke of it breathlessly and wide-eyed, as if she was my fairy godmother and this was her big chance to make me part of Black society in one fell swoop.

I loathed the idea of going but could not say no. Could not tell my Mom I had no interest in the artificiality of a formal ritual with a community of people I did not know. Could not remind her that I had a serious boyfriend with whom I'd much rather spend a fancy evening. She was trying so very hard to raise a Black child right. I didn't want to appear not to care about her efforts to salvage me.

Mom disassembled the bright red dress I'd worn in a madrigal group junior year and used her old Singer sewing machine to piece the fabric back together to resemble a ball gown. She bought some stiff rustling fabric that would go underneath the dress and protrude it outward from the waist like a cone. She commandeered my older brother Stephen to "escort" me. I was seventeen. Stephen was thirty-four.

In the late afternoon on the day of the event, resigned to the fact that I have to go to this thing, I do my makeup carefully, then press and press and re-press my hair to try to smooth it into some flippy swoopy design like I know the other Black girls will be sporting. I put on the black character shoes I wear for choir performances, pull on the stiff fabric that goes underneath the dress, and then finally I carefully step into the dress itself and my mother zips it. In the mirror I see that I'm playing a part in a play and am not sure I know my lines.

My brother Stephen arrives at the door in a tuxedo and hands me a corsage. My parents take a few pictures and soon we're off to Milwaukee, an hour and a half due east of Verona. We walk into the hotel lobby and I look around, desperate to find some face familiar from the Jack and Jill mall outing. But all I see is people who smile and laugh with one another and who do not smile and laugh with me. My hair begins its inevitable process of mushrooming into a pouf.

Stephen and I enter the grand ballroom and I make a beeline to an empty round table where I sit and catch my breath. Then I take in the scene swirling around me. Handsome boys in tuxedos dance with girls in elegant department-store dresses. A trio of girls with properly relaxed hair laugh at a food station. A young couple stands with their arms around each other at the foot of the elegant stairway that leads up to God knows where. I can't picture myself doing any of these things, me with my homemade dress, frizzy hair, and my grown man of a brother for a date. A cute boy walks confidently in my direction with a grin spreading across his face and I am about to smile and make eye contact when I see that his destination is a girl a few feet behind me. No one will ask me to dance that night and I already know it.

I go to a nearby food station and come back to our table with a plate loaded with savory hors d'oeuvres. I'm not used to feeling ugly, but that night I feel not only ugly but downright homely. Normally I'd be in clothes I liked and I'd have my hair in a ponytail and I'd look cute, cute enough for someone to date, cute enough to be on the Pompon team. I keep trying to smooth my hair down, pulling at the underneath bits near my ears, smoothing the entire back with the palm of my hand, absentmindedly trying to pull it back into a low bun only to remember and re-remember that I didn't even bring the always-have-on-hand hair tie that might now rescue me. It's like my hair is getting drunk and making a scene and I can't do a damn thing about it.

As the evening becomes a rousing party of rhythmic music punctuated by a voice on a microphone regularly announcing the next stage of this highly scripted debutante coming-out event, I fall rapidly to the bottom of the social ladder. Stephen asks me to dance because he also knows nobody is going to ask me. As we dance he doesn't make eye contact with me and instead gazes over the top of our outstretched clasped hands, which I presume is intended to preserve my dignity. But knowing that he too senses my dignity is falling apart at the seams feels like proof of it, and becomes the ultimate insult.

We return to our table and I keep looking at the black Swatch watch strapped to my wrist. I refuse Stephen's second and third requests to dance. I will the minutes to go by. Finally Stephen gives up and we sit there in silence. When it is nine thirty p.m. I feel we've been there long enough to prove I'd tried to participate, and I tell Stephen I want to go home.

We are largely silent on the long drive home and I cringe at the report he might give my parents. Of the failure at being a Black teenager I had been.

XXXI.

I'd told no one about my locker sign, and I'd go on to tell no one for decades. Not my parents, not the school administration, not my boyfriend Mark, not my best friend, Diana. For more than twenty years, though, the truth of that day hunkered down inside of me and metastasized.

I was the Nigger of my town.

DESPERATE TO BELONG

I.

College, I hoped, would be my chance to make Black friends, even learn how to "be Black." Whatever that would mean. If I was praying for anything in the summer of 1985, then I was praying for that to be true.

I hadn't had my hair cut by anyone but Mom since the disastrous cut in sixth grade that left me looking like a boy. But in the waning days of summer in Wisconsin, I walked into a white salon and asked the stylist to give me a short haircut like Lisa Bonet wore on *The Cosby Show*— no more than an inch long everywhere except the front, where I wanted it angled upward to form an overhang that would hover above my forehead, defying gravity.

I was preparing myself to join my new college community. I also wanted to go out for the crew team at Stanford—a sport I'd heard you could do without having done it in high school. The early morning workouts would demand easy hair. Something I could wet with the water from the sink, run a bit of gel through, and not have to worry about any longer.

As I watched the stylist snip my curls, watched my childhood hair fall to the floor, I saw the possibility of a new life awaiting where I wouldn't have to worry any longer.

II.

In September of 1985 my parents fly out to Stanford with me and help me move into my dorm, Branner Hall, home to 10 percent of the freshman class and predominantly white. In the late afternoon, we and my 160 dorm mates and their families gather in the huge lounge at the center of the first floor to hear a welcome talk from the faculty member who will be living with us in the dorm and supervising the dorm staff—History Professor Kennell Jackson. As I sit on the dark turquoise rug with my back against a white square column, my knees hugged to my chest, my eyes glued to Professor Jackson, I can't shake the question: What *is* he?

Kennell is in his midforties, tall, with a bit of a paunch protruding against his crisp white shirt and with enormous feet clad in leather dress shoes at the base of his khaki pants. He has an oblong head, a flat nose, twinkling eyes, and facial hair that covers the entire lower half of his face, sparse, but manicured like a putting green. He is balding, and where he has hair it is short and coiled like his facial hair, and blends well into his skin, which is reddish, like faded terra-cotta.

Kennell had walked to the front of the packed room in an aw-shucks, almost sheepish manner, *deliberately* casual though, I thought, as if the casualness was a carefully cultivated affect. I'd glanced over at my parents who stood against the far wall, and seen them exchange raised eyebrows and smiles with one another. Maybe they were having the same impression.

When Kennell begins to speak he keeps his elbows at his side and pats the air around him with the long fingers of his large hands, like a pianist plonking all ten fingers on the piano at once, and I hear in his Virginia drawl both words and sounds I'd never heard before. He tells us stories in fragments, and goes off on tangents, and just when I am wondering whether all of my professors in college will be this weird, he ties all of his thoughts together, masterfully. He closes with a look of mischief flashing across his face, eyes crinkling, lips pursed in a wide smile, explaining what we could expect in the coming year as if we students are embarking upon an unprecedented adventure together.

When Kennell finishes speaking we stand in clumps near him waiting to introduce ourselves. The lounge slowly empties, and I meet up with my parents in the dorm's courtyard to begin to say good-bye. I stand on my tippy toes to hug Daddy's tall frame, then lift my head up to receive his kiss as he lowers his head to touch his lips to mine. "You'll be okay, baby," he pronounces, putting his strong hands on my shoulders. I nod quickly and eke out a high-pitched "Yeah." In seventeen years I'd only seen Daddy cry once—when he was using a screwdriver and it slipped off the screw and plunged deep into the palm of his left hand. So as my sixty-seven-year-old father tears up under Palo Alto's cloudless blue sky surrounded by my new classmates and their parents outside of my new home, both he and I know to look away.

I turn to Mom, who, at five feet and half an inch, seems to be about half my father's height and is smiling wide. Any anguish she might have been feeling over sending her baby to college two thousand miles from home seems to have given way to a kind of glee—the same glee she'd shown when the kid almost fell over in his chair in the library at Dartmouth. It's her race strategy look. Her "We Gon' Be Okay" look. She throws her arms open and pulls me into her tight embrace. As she squeezes her final hug into me she whispers, giddily, "Isn't it great you have a Black Resident Fellow?"

It astounds me now to say it but I'd had no idea; until Mom told me Kennell was Black, I was the lightest-colored, most different-looking Black person I'd ever known. Daddy and Mom climb into their rental car and I wave and wave and wave until they drive out of sight. Walking back to my new so-called home, I feel uplifted. *Maybe if someone who looks like Professor Jackson belongs within Blackness, well maybe there's a bit of room for me in there too.*

III.

The Black community on the Stanford campus was approximately 6 percent of the undergraduate student body at that time, or about 450 students. During new student orientation, I see a flier for a welcome event sponsored by the Black Community Services Center and I decide to go.

I am nervous—conscious that I really only understand how to be myself among white people. Whites are not just what I am used to, they are really all I know. The event is being held at Stanford's African American theme dorm, Ujamaa, all the way across campus from my dorm. Walking up the front path to Ujamaa, I worry about whether I'll be accepted. Know how to behave. Know how—*who*—to be. How to be a real Black kid.

Through the multipaned window a bunch of kids are gathering. They look happy and comfortable like they might already know one another, even though that isn't possible. I pull open the heavy front door and head in the direction of the noise—the dorm lounge. There are a few empty chairs and spots available on couches but I don't feel like I should take one. I stand off toward a corner, my back against the wall.

There is music and laughter. An air of relaxation. Of exhale. I'd been to a lot of meetings over these first five days at Stanford and this one is by far the most warm. Yet I am overcome by a sensation of being out of place. I feel eyes glance on me, then just as quickly look away. None of these real Black kids has a white parent, I say to myself. None of them was the only Black kid in their high school.

Do I just feel out of place, or am I actually out of place? If I don't belong here, where do I belong?

A series of older students stand at the front of the lounge and proceed to tell us this and that about upcoming events and how to sign up for various clubs and organizations. After the presentations I will myself to go up to the sign-up table to put my name on the list for a few clubs, and while there, finally I try to engage one of the upperclassmen in a conversation. Trying so hard to connect, to be polite, to be liked, I can almost see his body recoil slightly when I speak, as if my effort to belong is so naked as to be pitiable.

I was the Blackest thing at Middleton High School, but having sat among real Black people for the past sixty minutes I'd learned I didn't have a clue about what mattered to Black people, or maybe even what it meant to *be* a Black person. The music they'd played at the outset was not familiar to me. We didn't have cable television out in Cherrywood, let alone a Black radio station; the only Black music I had listened to was Stacey's mixtape of Prince songs. The pop cultural references that made them laugh or nod in agreement were as meaningless to me as foreign words. They punctuated their conversations with shorthand and slang words, the ease of it like a secret code among them. And I'd learned from the few clues that had come my way in life so far that music, pop culture, and language were the things that were stereotypically Black. At this meeting I was like a kid climbing the ladder to a glorious fort I'd discovered hidden in the trees, and when I got to the top I could see kids playing through the window but when I put my hand on the doorknob, it was locked. *Could someone come and let me in*, my heart bleated, to no one.

Many years later I would learn that Blackness was less about skin color or hair or language and more, far more, about a lived, conscious committedness to issues that impact Black people, and I would accept my light-colored skin, the sound of my voice, the biracial kink of my hair. I would enter rooms of Black peers and have my smiles returned, and make conversation without feeling shame about my choice of words or manner of speech. I would learn that I had been wrong in perceiving that all Black people thought and acted the same way. And, having set those misperceptions aside, I would be able to locate myself within Blackness and make meaningful connections with Black people. Friends. And I would learn that all the years I thought I was being myself around white people had instead been more like a performance of the self. A performance designed to meet their approval, assuage their concerns, calm their fears, succeed at overcoming their negative judgment. I would one day fully embrace my Black self like a long-lost mother, hold myself in my own arms, singing "Sometimes I Feel Like a Motherless Child," whose lyrics were not meant for me but were nevertheless resoundingly true to my experience.

But on that day in 1985 as an almost eighteen-year-old, my mixed-race ancestry and white-community upbringing are, together, the enormous elephant in the room—perhaps only in my own head, perhaps in the minds of others—and I cannot get past it. Cannot see others around it. And therefore cannot be seen. I am in an unyielding one-way dialogue of apology for my ancestry. For my own existence. I am showing up as what I'd later learn Black people call an "Oreo"—Black on the outside but white on the inside; a label on one far end of the Black identity continuum that starts with Malcolm X and ends with Uncle Tom.

I walk back to my mostly white dorm feeling frantic. I'm not Black enough, and I'm certainly not white, not ever white.

I continue my hunt for clues about how to be. I continue to watch *The Cosby Show*, then its spin-off, *A Different World*, with my dorm mates on the large TV that always seems to be on in the Branner Hall lounge. Then, on January 28, 1986, we are watching the launch of the *Challenger* space shuttle and it blows up in our faces. And for some moments in time, race doesn't matter. We are all just grieving Americans.

IV.

Far from finding my community at college, I found myself on an island. Alone.

Who am I? Who decides that? Where do I belong? Do I belong anywhere? Do I exist at all if no group of humans will claim me?

As I search for familiarity and try to make new friends, these questions are my constant companions. These days of searching become weeks; the weeks become months, and the months become years. I make friends mostly with white people and with the small number of Black kids who also live in my dorm, row on the crew team, participate in theater, do student government, or take the pre-law classes. I would go back to Ujamaa just once in my time at Stanford for a study session in someone's dorm room. It was sophomore or junior year. Walking through the main hallway, I recognized a number of the brown faces and could smile and nod, but I didn't know anyone's name. And they did not know mine. I could not count them as friends. Although I now had more Black friends than in the aggregate years of my childhood— and other friends who were non-white—by staying away from Ujamaa I'd exiled myself from the heart of the Black community on campus.

V.

In November 1985 I turn eighteen. A world away from the familiarity of home, I become, legally, an adult. And as imperfect as the home of Verona, Wisconsin, had been for me, I feel a loss when I can no longer retreat there, to that place where, above all else, I knew my parents loved me. I am becoming a Black woman, treated in the world as such, and lacking the armor of self-love with which to withstand that treatment.

That winter, I bike with a handful of friends to the Stanford Shopping Center, a large shopping mall on the edge of campus which beckons with its expensive stores, gorgeous fountains, outdoor sculpture, and flowers in a perpetual bloom. The open-air pavilions ooze prestige, power, and exclusivity. The regular customers, the mostly white women I'd later come to know as "ladies who lunch," are a permanent part of the façade.

One friend had grown up in Palo Alto and while we are shopping she bumps into a woman she knows from childhood. We stand in our gaggle around the lady and our friend introduces us to her. When she gets to me, the lady takes note.

"Oh *you* go to Stanford too?" The sound of her voice is intrigue, wonder, even amazement.
"Yes."
"Oh! What team are you on?"

[The truth was I was a walk-on with the crew team.]
[The truth was, that's not what she was trying to get at.]

After we part ways with the lady, I try to laugh with my friends about it. "Can you believe she asked that?" I say casually, seeking their attention over the implied insult that I hadn't gotten into Stanford on my academic merits, and wanting to dismiss it as anomalous at the same time. Some of my friends get it, but not all.

As we make our way through the Stanford Shopping Center, my friends almost certainly forget about the incident, but it stays with me, lurking around every corner, staring back at me from every cosmetics counter mirror and every dressing-room wall.

In the aisles of the various department stores and boutiques, the store clerks' penetrating eyes seem to bore a hole in my back. I try to catch their eye and deliver a reassuring smile that says *I'm Black, but I'm not here to steal from you*, while smoothing my hair with my hand. But they either won't meet my eyes or no smile is returned. I begin to feel self-conscious about where I put my hands, whether I put them in my pockets or keep them free. I feel not only out of place but unwanted even, perhaps dirty, guilty of something, like my mere presence somehow lessens the value of their clothing, cosmetics, and shoes.

I'd signed up for a credit card from one of the many vendors hawking them at our campus student center. Desperate to refute a clerk's presumption that I am out of place in her store and perhaps up to no good, in the months and years to come I plunk that credit card down time after time after time at these expensive stores, spending more than I can afford to try to buy the certainty that I belonged. As if my purchases can refute their stereotypical assumptions: *I'm Black but have money! I'm Black but can afford to shop here! I belong here. See? I belong!*

For twenty-five years, as even my husband would come to know, even as I moved into the ranks of the upper middle class and held a position of some prominence in this very town, my steadfast rule was that I would never go to the Stanford Shopping Center unless I was dressed up, and specifically unless my hair was tame by white standards. For decades I worked hard to prevent those questions from coming. From ever penetrating me again.

VI.

Meanwhile, I am keeping a secret.

When in January I'd opened the envelope containing my first quarter grades, I saw a B, a C, and a D on my transcript. My 2.0 GPA was the proof I'd been expecting all along that people like me—Black, female, from the Midwest—in fact did not belong at a place like Stanford. To add insult to injury, the D was in Communications 1—the stereotypical "easy" class at any college.

If my grades get even a hairsbreadth worse, I could flunk out of Stanford.

VII.

On a routine call with my parents in February Daddy asks, "Baby, how'd it go fall quarter?" I begin to cry, and spill the truth, and relief washes over me. It's the volume of reading, I tell them—so many texts to get through really quickly—and papers longer than I'd ever had to write at Middleton High. Daddy and Mom hold on to me over the phone. Tell me they love me. Tell me I can do it. Tell me I have what it takes to succeed. Urge me to go get help.

I get help—ironically, from the very academic advising office I would manage twenty-five years later as dean—from an advisor who asks me about my habits, then tells me that I have what it takes intellectually but my study skills and time management need a lot of help. And she strongly urges me not to choose classes based on what "everyone" is taking and instead to take classes that sound interesting to me. When spring quarter starts in late March, I flip through the course catalog and find a class that sounds right up my alley.

It is a political science class that will survey the history of the doctrines of civil rights and civil liberties in America. The texts look engaging and rigorous. The format is going to be Supreme Court case studies, which excites me because I think I might want to go to law school. And the professor—a young white guy named Jim Steyer—is already peppering his lectures with war stories about his time at the NAACP Legal Defense Fund in New York. And he is cute. Which doesn't hurt. By midway through the quarter every one of the two hundred students in that class know we'd stumbled upon something special. And I, to my great *relief*, am managing the very intense workload, keeping up with assignments, and making analytical connections at a pretty deep level. I can feel my body healing from the wounds of intellectual inadequacy inflicted by the first quarter.

VIII.

A few weeks earlier, *The Color Purple* had vied for the Academy Award for Best Picture. Alice Walker's Pulitzer Prize–winning novel was now in the hands of blockbuster director Steven Spielberg, and the cast included Danny Glover, as well as new faces on the film screen—Oprah Winfrey and Whoopi Goldberg. They'd received eleven nominations in all for this violent, haunting, exquisitely sad, redemptive depiction of the lives of Black women. But the white woman's African journey *Out of Africa*, which began with Meryl Streep saying, "I had a farm in Ahf-ree-kah," won the day. *The Color Purple* would tie for the dishonor of having the most Oscar nominations without a single win. Two years later, a film about a white woman who got chauffeured everywhere by a Black man played by Morgan Freeman would get the Oscar: *Driving Miss Daisy*.

IX.

Later that spring, Professor Steyer asks a very tough question in our civil rights class, which was not unusual. What is unusual is that I know exactly what he is getting at and I ache to respond. But to date I'd never raised my hand in a class at Stanford and still don't dare to do so. Besides this is obviously a really complicated question—no one else is raising their hand. My fear of being wrong, of being *Black* and wrong, silences me even though I know I have a good idea here. Scanning the huge room for potential volunteers, Steyer glances at me. Something in my face must be showing him my brain is working overtime. He nods once at me and raises his eyebrows, signaling that I should speak up. "Well," I begin, clearing my throat and playing with my hair. And then I keep on talking.

Steyer, never one to downplay a dramatic moment, folds his arms across his chest, leans back on one heel, and starts nodding his head vigorously as I talk. So I keep going. My classmates—watching the clear evidence in Steyer's behavior that I am saying good stuff—begin scribbling down what I am saying. I am teaching my classmates. I am speaking from a place grounded in knowledge and bolstered by confidence. With a voice pushing through the brambles out into the clearing.

This is the starting line of my efforts to be better than whites expect a Black person can be. A race I'll run—and try to win—for the next twenty years.

X.

Have I mentioned my roommates? They are a white girl from a very wealthy family in Queens, New York, and a well-to-do Thai girl from Bangkok who goes by the nickname Pinkie. The roommate from Queens tells me her older brother likes to joke that one of us is "Pinkie" and the other is "Blackie."

XI.

"Screw Your Roommate" is an old Stanford tradition. Your dorm throws a party and your roommate sets you up with a blind date from another dorm. When it comes time for Screw Your Roommate in the spring of my freshman year, my roommates pore over the book of pictures of the entire freshman class to find a boy suitable for me.

They point out a picture of a boy in a neighboring dorm. He doesn't look particularly attractive. And from the way they'd skipped from Black face to Black face as they perused the pages of the book, it is clear the only reason they'd chosen him for me was race. It's a throwback to Daddy's old joke about Bates College admitting one Black woman to complement the one Black man in each class, "so they'll have someone to date." Back in the 1930s. And the deliberate race-matching feels like me and Frederick all over again, except this time the matchup is being done to me instead of the other way around.

Inside my head I am screaming what I cannot say, which is, "Wait, aren't I good enough for a white boy?"

I go to the party with this boy who is nice enough but who seems about as interested in me as I am in him. It is impossible to know whether we might have had an interest in each other had the sole reason for our being thrown together in the first place not been race. Had the circumstances not seemed so presumptive, racist, offensive, I might have been able to enjoy myself. And him.

XII.

That first summer after college I return to Wisconsin and live with my parents for the last time.

Mom is a student in her own right now, pursuing at UW Madison the PhD she'd interrupted when Daddy's work took us from Madison to Reston, Virginia, back in 1977. I know I have to get a job, and look through the classified section of the *Wisconsin State Journal* to find one. I never dreamed of asking Daddy if I could have a job in his office—the kind of gig many of my college classmates were getting that summer.

I come across corn de-tasseling—a sort of quintessential Wisconsin job that entails walking up and down the rows of corn and removing the pollen-producing tassel from the top of each plant and dropping it to the ground, a manner of cross-pollination. It pays minimum wage, $3.35 per hour.

I show up for work on the outskirts of some farm and ride with ten or so other people—all male, all white—in the back of a truck that threatens to jostle us back and forth and into each other as we make our way out to the crop. But I am strong from rowing crew and can keep my body rigid as the ride tosses us around.

I march up and down the rows de-tasseling the stalks with little fatigue. On our water breaks and lunch break my coworkers eye me with uncertainty. I keep to myself. I hadn't realized that I should protect myself from the sun and instead had worn a tank top and shorts because of the heat. At the end of the first day I am considerably darker head to toe and the skin on either side of my tank top straps is blistered a purple brown.

At the end of the second day my coworkers and I come in from the field and stand where the crops end and the dirt road leading back to the main road begins. We form a circle around the foreman, who is telling us what we'll tackle tomorrow. The truck to take us out sits idling. I wipe the sweat from my forehead with the back of my hand, look at the wet dark slime that accumulated there, and have an epiphany. I need to work. But I don't need to do *this* work. I am a high school graduate, which means I have more options. I quit and get paid right there on the spot: a gross wage of $53.60 netting me $35.90.

I improve my working conditions tremendously by becoming a bus girl at Perkins, a twenty-four-hour diner franchise one step up from a Denny's. I wear a brown skirt, a white blouse with a little brown tie, and a white ruffled apron. My job is to clear, clean, and set tables and mop the bathroom floors. This job also pays $3.35 an hour. But I had moved from the fields to a building where I can go to the bathroom whenever I need to. I shower when I get home, but when Mark and I make out I still smell a bit like fried food.

Early one evening before the dinner rush begins I am walking through the aisles with my gray dirty-dishes bin and pass a Black male customer seated at a table with two other folk. He calls me over. "Aren't you George Lythcott's daughter?" I say yes and smile and make chitchat and he fills in details for his companions. He asks me where I go to college and I tell him. Then I nod in the direction of my manager who is coming toward me, and I sidle over to the nearest table that needs clearing. I put the gray bin on the Formica tabletop and begin piling dishes in.

"She doesn't have to do this work, you know," I hear the customer tell my white manager as I'm wiping the table down. "She'll be a sophomore at Stanford." I feel a strange discomfort as he says this, like I've been outed. I couldn't have explained it then, but I was trying to prove something with this job. I wanted to punch a clock, work hard, and get a paycheck. I already felt an unease from being able to flit through life using my parents' name or that of the university I attended. I didn't want to be given unearned things. A summer spent wearing a uniform and earning minimum wage was a chance to pay some dues that many people who look like me had no choice but to pay.

Yet through my unease I can also hear in his voice that this stranger is happy for me. Proud of me. Proud that I am lifting myself and by extension *all of us* up and away from this kind of work. He sees me not as a white-talking biracial girl but as a Black kid *making* it. Maybe the commendation from the College Board wasn't that inaccurate after all.

XIII.

Right before I am to head back to college for the start of sophomore year, Mark leaves on his two-year Mormon mission—a veritable exile from family and friends. I get invited to a party hosted by one of the Black kids in Madison I'd met through Jack and Jill. There, I meet a boy. He is a little darker than me, and a little taller, with trim facial hair and an interest in politics. In conversation about current events with four or five other people, we prove to each other that we care about the same things. We then joke at a level the others don't get. At the end of the evening he asks me out.

We make a date for the following Thursday. This was a real boy-asking-me-out-because-he-likes-me situation, not a racially based prom ask or a consolation prize or a blind date.

We go out. Dinner? A movie? All I remember is being in his car in the hour before my curfew. I felt the need to do things without being asked. To take the initiative. Be aggressive. Be into it. We began kissing. Touching. I felt him through his jeans, unzipped them, and leaned over.

I didn't know where this would go, if anywhere, and it did in fact go nowhere. I barely thought of him again. But I could finally stop berating myself for never having gone out with a Black guy. I used him. Maybe he was using me, too.

XIV.

In the fall of sophomore year, I make the cast of a campus musical, and at rehearsal one day I have trouble mastering a dance step. This embarrasses me. For solace I turn to another Black girl in the cast and gasp in mock self-deprecation, "I should be better at this— I'm Black!" The girl stares at me in cold silence, then abruptly turns away and strides off into the wings, glancing back at me once with an unmistakable look of disgust. I stand there, stammering and gesticulating with my hands, trying to explain what I had really meant.

What did I really mean?

XV.

I fill my course schedule sophomore year with classes in American history, literature, and government on my way to an American Studies major, which not only nourishes me intellectually in a way I'd never experienced before but also provides a foundation for the law degree I plan to pursue after college.

Professor Steyer picks me to be one of only two sophomores in an upper-level seminar on civil rights. We are assigned a case to brief and debate, and I choose *Drummond v. Fulton County Department of Family and Children's Services*, a case of white foster parents, the Drummonds, seeking to adopt the mixed-race boy they'd been raising since he was one month old.

The case pulls hard on my heart—the white parents, on the one hand, claiming that they can love and raise this Black boy to a healthy and whole adulthood, the Black social workers, on the other hand, claiming that the boy needs to be raised in the Black community by Black parents. The social workers are effectively saying that someone like me could be harmed by being raised in a white community. I could not bear the possible truth of the truth of this so I take the side of the Drummonds.

When I finish my oral argument and get my written brief back, I have two important pieces of feedback from Steyer:

    1) Your oral advocacy is fantastic.
    2) Your writing needs *a lot* of work.

XVI.

American studies.

The rules of America as freshly written in 1787 classified my ancestors as chattel—property of a white man—and as three-fifths of a person for political representation purposes. Having it both ways, to suit the white men who ran the South. Later, after the Civil War and the unmet promise of Reconstruction, the laws and policies of America treated us like stray dogs—expecting us to be content with the scraps that America was generous enough to throw our way, tolerating us but not entitling us to come inside the house—or, at least, asking us to remain content with entering through the back door.

This was hardly news to me. The imperfect nature of our so-called union—the unmet promise of "liberty and justice for all"—were playing in the background of my American childhood. The miniseries *Roots*, which came out when I was ten. The strident conversations between my parents and their liberal friends over cocktails or a barbecue. Daddy's tales of his Jim Crow childhood and young adulthood. My older siblings' accounts of civil rights activism. My mother forcing an indifferent school to test me for giftedness. The debates over school busing, voting rights, and affirmative action that made appearances on the nightly news. Also on the news? The Klan. One night as a child of maybe eight or nine, as I sat with my parents for their evening ritual of watching Walter Cronkite, I saw a cross burning, saw hordes of people with white sheets for robes, white masks with holes cut for eyes, saw a child, someone younger than I was, dressed like that.

But becoming a student of these issues—studying the work of historians, reading Supreme Court decisions, comprehending that the Reagan administration and the Rehnquist Court were rolling back the government's commitment to redressing past discrimination in voting, employment, housing, and college admission—left me heavy with ache. I believed in America right up until then.

Now I felt severed from a love I would never again feel.

Motherless.
Homeless.

America.
I'd thought she wanted me.

XVII.

"Hey-hey, ho-ho. Western Culture's got to go!"

I chant that with the Reverend Jesse Jackson when he comes to campus to support our protest of the university's freshman humanities core requirement: Western Culture, which features only the work of dead white men. Hundreds of us, students of every hue and gender, march with Jesse under his Rainbow Coalition flag. We are the inheritors of the civil rights struggle of his youth. It is our turn to weave some new threads into the American tapestry and narrative.

The faculty senate votes to replace Western Culture with Cultures, Ideas, and Values, which comes with a more diverse set of texts. Reagan's secretary of education, William Bennett, takes to the *Wall Street Journal* to excoriate Stanford's president, Don Kennedy, for caving to multiculturalists. A few students found the *Stanford Review* to provide a counter-perspective steeped in conservatism and libertarianism. Looking over my shoulder before doing so, I subscribe.

XVIII.

I am under the influence of many things in college, including:

Malcolm X: teaching separation over integration as the way to our salvation, as adamant about the need for separation of the races as any racist white man.

Amiri Baraka: mocking me in "Poem for HalfWhite College Students" . . . *when you find yourself gesturing like Steve McQueen, check it out, ask / in your black heart who it is you are, and is that image black or white* . . .

The *Stanford Review*: spelling out my enemy's blueprints and battle plans. But why the annual subscription when I could pick it up from a newspaper kiosk? I tell myself it's because I believe in free speech and their right to exist. But years later, when I can finally interrogate this self, I realize I subscribed because I was scared to death of these unhooded whites printing their disdain for our existence. I thought *well if I'm on their subscriber list maybe they'll leave me alone.*

The Mormon Church: preaching a different kind of salvation. I visit every Sunday morning by walking out of my dorm and turning left, a twenty-minute walk to a building where I learn how to pray to a God who discriminated against Black men until 1978 and I learn the Missionaries' lessons (although I stop reading the *Book of Mormon* on page 66 where it says a tribe of people were cursed with a skin of blackness) and when they ask if I am ready to be baptized I say yes and in spring of 1987 I am baptized in a full-water immersion ceremony and at Christmas later that year I will announce to my parents and half siblings that I have joined the Mormon Church and their jaws will drop and their mouths will fill with silence and for once in my life I will have this family's complete attention.

I am an island.
I am on an island.
My family abandoned me on this island.
And I will not be judged.

XIX.

The summer after sophomore year I hold an internship in Washington, D.C., with a public interest law firm located on E Street near Union Station. One of their side projects is DC Statehood, a movement to end the systemic disenfranchisement of DC residents—most of whom are Black—who are taxed by the federal government but have no voting representation in the House of Representatives or the Senate. I attend meetings with impassioned activists, draft language to help our cause, and, of course, I do the obligatory intern things like get coffee and run errands.

One day one of our attorneys leaves something behind at the office and, like any good intern, I volunteer to run back and get it. But I am in a pencil skirt and heels so it is more like a march than a run. Making my way up E Street, I hear the voice of a stranger behind me. "I hope you don't mind my saying this, but you have gorgeous calves." The voice is warm, soft. I know my calves are strong from rowing crew. My quads and biceps, too. I turn around and see a Black man, smiling. I blush. Smile. Thank him. Turn around and keep walking. And keep smiling. This wasn't a creepy whistle from a construction site. I don't feel assaulted by his words. I feel seen.

XX.

The room I sublet that sweltering summer is in a house that has seen better days. Roaches, no air-conditioning, and seventeen roommates in all—mostly students from Stanford and Duke—in a house meant for a single family. The four bedrooms, basement, and sun porch are crammed with our bodies and belongings.

It is 1987, and one particular night a group of us are up late sitting in the hallway on the second floor, talking about President Reagan's decision to slash funds for low-income housing and mental health services, which created what we know thirty years later to be a permanent class of homeless people. Even late in the evening the air is hot and thick with humidity, and fans blast at either end of the crowded hall. Our rhetoric soon turns from criticizing the President to boasting about what we would do if we were President one day. At which point a fellow Stanford classmate turns to me.

"Well at least you don't have to worry about that," he says with a smile.
"Hmmm?"
"You can't be President. You were born in Nigeria."
"But I've always been an American citizen. I've never been anything else."
"Sorry," he says, cutting me off. *Was it smugness I saw on his white face or just the confidence that comes from certainty?* He looks away.

I scramble to my feet, step over the legs of the students sprawled on the carpeted floor, and walk briskly down the hall to my room. I know exactly where to find the pocket-sized copy of the U.S. Constitution I keep among my political science and history textbooks. I grab it off the shelf and begin flipping through it, searching for the section I know holds the answer. By the time I get back to my housemates splayed on the carpet, I am quoting aloud from Article II:

No person except a natural born Citizen, or a Citizen of the United States, at the time of the Adoption of this Constitution, shall be eligible to the Office of President . . .

"That's me," I say, tapping the page. "Natural Born. My dad's American and I've never had any citizenship other than American." To me the question was asked and answered. And to my friend as well.

"Sorry, Julie," he says, shaking his head. "Nope. You're not Natural Born."

It was impossible to know that evening who was right. The Supreme Court had not weighed in on whether the requirement "Natural Born" applied to someone like me—born to an American citizen outside the U.S. That question would rear its head on a national stage in 2008 when the Birther Movement arose around the question of Barack Obama's citizenship (despite his birth in Hawaii and his mother's American citizenship), and arose again in 2015 with presidential candidate Senator Ted Cruz having been born in Canada to an American mother and a Cuban father.

But all of that was decades off, unknowable to me or to my fellow interns that sticky evening. This was a conversation among young adults about our wishes and dreams, and I read in my Stanford classmate's declaration not just a statement of fact he believed to be true, but judgment. As if I, already of lower status by virtue of my Blackness, was lowered yet again having been born in the wrong place.

XXI.

One Sunday morning junior year, just weeks after I tell my family I'd joined the Mormon Church, I go to church for the last time.

It's a special service held every now and again where, without warning, the Bishop calls upon a handful of congregants to give a personal testimonial. I am instantly terrified. I know my conversion was half-assed—I'd read less than a quarter of the *Book of Mormon* because of its line on Blackness but I'd said yes to baptism because the lessons were over and it seemed the inevitable next step and then there's the matter of this boy Mark who introduced me to all of this whom I still love. Now I find myself seated on a pew among real Mormons and I can't shake the nagging feeling that I am going to be called. I don't think I can B.S. my way through it. I start to feel queasy.

The first person begins to speak and I search my mind for scripture that I can thread with my life experience to make some kind of coherent story. The person finishes and the Bishop glances around the room to decide whom to call next. I avoid eye contact by bending to examine the heel of my left shoe. He calls the second person. *Phew, not me.* Then the third. I look at my watch. Twelve minutes to go. *Please God let him not call me.* I spend those final twelve minutes half searching for what I might say and half praying this third person will take all the remaining time.

The service ends, and relief courses through my body. I practically bound down the aisle toward the main door where the Bishop stands saying good-bye to worshippers. He stops me gently with his hand. Looks at me. Smiles.

"Julie, you were next, you know."

I did know. I knew it so deeply in my soul that it frightened me. I was so frightened that I never went back.

XXII.

A few months later, I start dating a white, Jewish boy named Dan. His wry humor and gentle manner had made him a fast friend. The mutual attraction is clear by spring. And his handwritten letters mailed every single day over the following summer cement the bond. Dan is now my life partner of close to thirty years. But back at the start we both had family who might try to stand in the way.

In June 1988 Dan and I drive across the country from Stanford to the New York area where my parents had relocated, and where Dan's mother as well as his father and stepmother live. It's a meet-the-parents road trip times three. After the long drive we stop at my folks' place first. I take the steps tentatively toward a house I've never visited before, my new boyfriend in hand.

I know my parents might be disappointed that Dan is white. My mom's fervent, frequently expressed hope that I would have more Black friends despite living in a white town is always in the back of my mind. But they are an interracial couple themselves, and I'm not going to let them balk at the racial difference between me and Dan. My far greater concern is Dan's Jewishness. My childhood was peppered with Daddy's jokes about Jews and other ethnic groups.

Twenty minutes after we arrive at my folks' place, Daddy has sized up Dan. He walks me out of the living room and into the hallway, turns to me, puts his strong finger under my chin, and lifts my face up to meet his aging, watery eyes. Daddy is now seventy years old.

"It's clear he adores you. That's all that matters to me."

XXIII.

Daddy was right. Dan adored me, and three decades later he does still. He loved me when in my deepest self-loathing over being both too Black for whites and not Black enough for Blacks I couldn't even locate a self with which to love myself.

XXIV.

Three decades later I also know that the whiteness of my future spouse was the inevitable outcome of the inertia of those young adult years in which I went after the approval of white strangers from store clerks to faculty to bosses. A white boy, a white *husband* was the route to the destination I desperately craved without even knowing it: belonging in America.

XXV.

Dan himself was not inevitable. He was a gift.

XXVI.

Dan and I lived in the same dorm. One day that first spring together, before we'd ever introduced each other to our parents, I emerge from the girls' shower on my hall and bump into him. I am wearing a yellow robe and flip-flops, and am gripping my shower caddy. My hair is dripping wet; the corkscrew curls I had not yet blown straight with a hair dryer and pressed smooth with a curling iron are dangling about my head. And while I usually wear a full face of makeup, my skin is bare. Not exactly the way I want to be seen by my new boyfriend.

"You have curly hair." A strange look like bemusement spreads across his face. The memory of white boys teasing me over my hair in high school comes surging back.

"Yeah?" I step back and clutch my robe to my body. I just want to scurry back to my room, shut the door, and emerge when I look presentable. Pretend this whole thing never happened.

"I love it."

What? You wait what?
Damn.

XXVII.

Senior Year. Thanksgiving 1988. Dan is in Florida. I am at my parents' home in New York, waiting for their phone to ring.

Dan's family is gathered for the holiday. Some months ago Dan sent a picture of us to Nana, his grandmother, and his family has heard about it, and they know that what Nana saw in the picture was not a nice girl standing with her grandson but a *schvartze*, and now everyone is wondering what Nana will say or do when she sees Dan in person.

As a dozen of Dan's family members watch Dan approach the indomitable family matriarch, I sit by the phone in my parents' home, awaiting word, awaiting word that it went okay, that he is okay, that I am okay, hoping he'll say not just that it went okay but that someone in his family finally stood up to this woman instead of making him stand there alone.

XXVIII.

Three weeks later, Dan and I head home for the winter holidays. His father and stepmother throw their annual Christmas party in their Manhattan apartment. My parents are invited, and Dan and I ride to the party in their car. We arrive at the building amid a throng of partygoers who announce breezily to the doorman "Bruce and Judy's." The doorman nods, then gestures to the bank of elevators to the right. However, when Daddy walks through the door, the doorman takes a large step toward him and holds his hand up like a stop sign. I watch Daddy's lips curl in anger as he meets the eyes of this working-class white man. I dart my eyes from Daddy to Dan, who quickly steps up and says, "No. I'm Bruce's son. We're going up." My twenty-year-old white Jewish boyfriend opens a door closed to my seventy-year-old Black father.

XXIX.

Later that evening, I meet Dan's stepsister Emily for the first time.

Emily, a fourteen-year-old white girl not very comfortable hanging out with the Manhattan socialites filling her mother's foyer and living room, is hiding out in her bedroom. That's where, after a half hour of knowing each other, Emily confides a story to me.

"I was raised by a Black nanny named Cathy," she begins. "And one day when I was in kindergarten, I got sent home early . . ."

For her entire young life Emily had attended elite independent schools on the Upper West Side in Manhattan. One day when she was in kindergarten her teacher had asked the children what they wanted to be when they grew up. "A fire truck," Emily answered. The teacher explained to Emily that she couldn't be a fire truck, she had to be some kind of *person*. "Okay, then I want to be Black." The teacher said that wasn't possible. "Then I want to be a boy!" The teacher pointed out that this too was impossible. Five-year-old Emily was inconsolable over not being able to achieve any of the things she wanted to become, and the teacher called home. Emily waited on the little cot in the nurse's office. Cathy appeared and held her tight.

In an American literature class at Stanford that fall, I'd read Toni Morrison's *The Bluest Eye*. I'd related to the little Black girl protagonist who was intrigued by white dolls with blue eyes, but I'd had trouble with the scene about a little white girl seeking refuge in the arms and body of her Black housekeeper. A white girl finding succor in a Black mother figure? I had never heard of such a thing. Could not even imagine it. Before reading Toni Morrison, I had never even read about it in fiction.

Now I'm sitting in the bedroom of a real white girl—a white girl who'd grown up amid considerable privilege in New York—who wanted to be Black? *What can this white girl see about Black people that I can't see? How can she want to be me more than I do?*

I had never felt the embrace of a Black mother.
I knew of no comfort like Cathy's arms.

XXX.

That June, I graduate from college. The last paper I write is for John Manley's class, The American Dream. Manley is a Marxist. He isn't the first professor to assign me *The Autobiography of Malcolm X*, but he is the first to force me to confront my own role in my alienation from both America and Black America. I title my paper "Buying into the American Dream—Is It Worth the Price?" It begins:

> *I sit here at my desk, a soon-to-be-graduating senior at Stanford University, trying to reduce the pile of clutter that covers my desktop in hopes that this will somehow help unclutter my mind. Most of the correspondence can be chucked into a throwaway pile, or can be neatly filed away. But not this particular letter. When I first received it, it angered and frustrated me, and now its presence fills me with remorse as I'm forced to examine the truth about my upbringing. The letter? An invitation to the Black Baccalaureate Ceremony for graduating seniors. The problem? A lifetime of standing on the outskirts of the Black community has taught me that I'm not Black enough to attend.*

Rereading this college paper today at close to fifty years of age, holding in my hands the words of my twenty-one-year-old self articulating a concern I'd spend the next twenty years trying to unwind, leaves me breathless. At first it feels like my younger self has made a trip through time to remind me what was clear even then amid what felt like muddy terrain inside me.

I did not attend that Black Baccalaureate Ceremony in 1989. While I had been somewhat politically active as a student, and had met Black student leaders through those efforts, I hadn't attended parties thrown by Black students and had all but exiled myself from Ujamaa. I could not fathom bringing my light brown, white-sounding self to the graduation gathering, not to mention my white mother, whose existence vis-à-vis me and the Black community was becoming an embarrassment to me.

When my parents arrive for graduation, Mom sees the Black Baccalaureate listed in the schedule of weekend activities and asks in a hopeful tone if we'll be going, and I answer her with an angry look. I blame her for my exile, blame her for creating a child who has no sense of belonging to the only people who might possibly claim her as theirs.

XXXI.

That college paper reads less like a time capsule I'm delighted to have unearthed and more like a tomb that was best left buried:

> *There was a time . . . when I avoided associating with other blacks, when I tried to emphasize my HALF WHITE/half black status and when I was ashamed to be seen with my daddy.*

These feelings about Daddy I don't recall ever feeling despite all I do recall are memorialized in the fading 12-point ink letters of a dot-matrix printer and he is gone now has been gone for twenty-one years and I am ashamed God I am so ashamed not of him but of myself to have felt shame toward this beautiful man for even one fleeting second.

These words. Like quicksand. A trap. Like a truth that swallows itself.

XXXII.

Manley's class was a mirror that showed me things about myself I hadn't seen before. I'd known race and racism and America's preference for whites and whiteness erected a wall between me and whites demarcating white as normal and me as other. But the wall between me and Blacks was there too, though harder to put my hands on or see. Manley's class forced me to see that the higher socioeconomic class that comes with professional success—the access to the good schools, the access to homes in white towns that can come with such status—

if one so chooses—

is a form of passing out of otherness out of darkness into lightness into whiteness.

I did not choose it. No one asked. But there's no question these choices lifted me. And if asked, I'd have said yes lift me with these opportunities. Just maybe not this far.

As loathsome as it was to learn that the engine of the American Dream itself—capitalism—was the invisible hand guiding me away from a people, a community, a tradition, at least now I understood the source of much of my dislocation and unbelonging. That being upper middle class had given me more in common with upper-middle-class whites than with middle-class or working-class or poor Blacks. I graduated from college knowing I was not some freak of nature but an easily predicted data point in our macroeconomic system.

XXXIII.

Dan was a few years behind me in school, so I worked on campus the year following my graduation while waiting for him to finish his degree. I worked at the public service center, in a yearlong position that was always filled by a recent grad. The center's mission was to get more undergraduates to do community service and to commit themselves more broadly to a life of public and community service.

At the start of the new school year I am invited to speak at RA Training—the training for the two hundred or so residential assistants who will serve on staffs in undergraduate dorms in the coming school year. I'd served for two years as a resident assistant on Kennell's staff—regarded by many as the most plum of RA assignments—and it was an honor to be selected as the former RA who would stand at a podium and offer the next crop of campus leaders whatever advice I could muster.

Following my talk, a residence dean named Greg Ricks stands up to announce the next item on the agenda: a workshop on institutional racism. Since RAs work with and support students of all backgrounds, the workshop is a chance to dive deep into some of the research on structural inequality, how to bridge differences, and how to create a space where everyone could be heard. Dean Ricks invites me to stay if I want. I want.

The people setting up the workshop tape six huge pieces of paper to the walls of the large room, demarcating the gathering point for each different racial group. Dean Ricks tells us to go sit by the sign with which we most identify, and talk amongst ourselves about how it feels to be there in that group. We should take notes, he says, because afterward we will gather again as a whole and report out.

I scan the room for the signs and see "White," "Asian," "Chicano/ Latino," "Native American." Finally I find the sign that says "Black" and begin to walk toward it. Some folks I know and like are already gathering there. I can choose that. I've always chosen that label, even when the arbiters of Blackness didn't choose me. But as I walk, I see the sixth and final sign: "Mixed/Other." Dean Ricks's instructions pound in my head. "Sit by the sign with which you most identify." I am being given a way to acknowledge my white mother.

What the hell? What the hell.

The mere existence of that sign feels transgressive. Political. Fraught. But it beckons me. I take a deep breath and look from side to side to see who might be noticing the choice I am about to make. I walk toward it.

There are two, maybe three people over there already and they don't look a thing like me. Except for their hair that doesn't match their nose that doesn't match their eyes that doesn't match their lips or the color of their skin. I sit down. A few more students join. There are maybe seven of us in all out of a group of two hundred. The instructions are to sit with our group and write down specific words describing what it feels like to be in a same-race group. But we have a hard time following this instruction because we can hardly get over the fact of our own coexistence.

After about fifteen minutes, Dean Ricks calls us back together to report out on what the prior exercise had felt like. The Black students share words like "safe," "family," "belonging," and "home." The White students say things like "normal," "plain," "why," and "oppressor." When it's time for my group to share our words, we glance around at each other and make strange faces and shrug our shoulders, knowing our words are very different from everything else we've just heard. Our words are "wow," "cool," and "never had this chance before."

After all the groups report out, Ricks tells us to go back to those same-race groups and talk some more. I return to the "Mixed/Other" sign and sit on the ground underneath it and begin talking with the others. We pause as one new person, then another, and another come toward us—people who'd previously sat in the "Black," "Chicano/Latino," and "Asian" groups. About two minutes in, a person comes over from the White group and says "I think I actually belong here." It happens again. And again. By the end of this session, our group has more than doubled in size. Close to twenty people look around at each other and take in the sameness of our myriad differences. People tear up a bit. I may have been one of them. No one is laughing, pointing, or scoffing at us. Or maybe they are but we don't know it. Or maybe we just don't need to look around to find out. We talk about what it is like to be mixed. We nod our heads at each other's stories. We mutts that didn't seem to fit anywhere else have each other *because* of our deviations from some so-called normal. For an hour that afternoon, we feel powerful. Empowered. We are outing ourselves as mixed-race people.

XXXIV.

The movie *Glory* came out in December of 1989 to high critical and popular acclaim. The story tells of an all-Black regiment of Civil War soldiers who fought for the Union, and starred Morgan Freeman, Denzel Washington, and Matthew Broderick. Dan and I go one night, and as I sit there in the Cineplex getting drawn deeper and deeper into the drama, something hibernating way down deep in me begins to wake that night. I cannot make the feeling go away.

The story in *Glory* was not an epiphany. It was just a well-told, well-acted depiction of what it was like to have been a slave, to be freed, to fight for a United States that did not see you as equal, and paid you less than a white even though you wore the same uniform. To fight for a nation whose countrymen called you Nigger.

I was not seeing new things on that screen. I was seeing with eyes that could see more clearly, maybe because now that I'd located a place for myself within Blackness—biracial—I could also locate a place for myself in the larger Black narrative.

Light-skinned mixed-race Black with a white-sounding voice? Yes, and

These are your people.

These are my people. These who suffered so that I could live a life and I have lived a far better life than most. A crystal stair.

What you gonna do about it?

In the theater that night I feel empathy for my ancestors, gratitude for the progress made by prior generations of Black Americans, sheepishness, even some shame for my unearned privilege, and an impulse to do something. To continue the progress of the Black community.

XXXV.

Senior year I'd been too busy with my classes, my responsibilities to the residents on my hall, and my work as a senior class president to apply for law school. I make up for lost time by studying hard for the LSAT and filling out law school applications. I write my personal statement about biracial identity, Black consciousness, and the experience I'd had watching *Glory* (despite advice from my brother Stephen—a lawyer—who says the essay is too politically risky). In April, I get the incredible news that I am admitted to Harvard Law School. I hunger for the legitimacy a degree from a prestigious East Coast institution will confer upon me.

One of my colleagues at the Haas Center for Public Service had been a Freedom Rider in the summer of 1961. Another would go on to found AmeriCorps. They had taken and were taking paths toward what was good and right rather than toward prestige and money. I don't know whether my colleagues will be impressed or disappointed by my law school news. As word about my intended destination spreads among them, I clarify that I am going because it's a good degree to have and that I'll be doing public service work after I graduate.

I feel genuinely relieved when one of my colleagues, Izzy, claps me on the back and beams over my law school news. Izzy is an older white woman in her fifties who doesn't suffer fools gladly. I am intimidated by her. She knows a lot about a lot of things and her opinion matters to me.

A few weeks after I commit to Harvard, Izzy's husband, Jack, comes to visit the office. He's a retired judge and I know from the way our colleagues speak of him with reverence in their voice that he's had a storied career. I presume he'll be impressed by my law school news. Maybe see us as cut from the same cloth. Maybe, if I make a decent connection with him, he'll help me find a clerkship with a judge when the time comes. I walk across the hall to Izzy's office to meet her husband and feel nervous excitement rising inside me.

Izzy's husband is not what I expected. With his big beard, barrel chest, and stocky legs, he looks more like Santa Claus than like a judge. Izzy introduces us and saves the news about my admittance to Harvard Law School for last, savoring the telling of it like a crescendo. She's proud of me, I can tell.

The judge reacts by leaning his stout body toward me to look me straight in the eye. Then he sinks back on his heels, spreads his arms wide, and guffaws, "Oh, so you're a twofer!" He grabs me by the hand and pulls me out of his wife's office and races ahead of me down the stairs, shouting back at me over his shoulder. "Let's see if you can pass this test." I am good at tests. I have no idea what he's talking about, but as I hit the ground floor I am cautiously excited.

He grabs my hand again as we exit the building and he leads me out to the parking lot. Izzy is bringing up the rear, shouting, "Jack!" She sounds exasperated and apologetic, like a person whose dog likes to sniff people between the legs. The judge walks me over to an old rusty pickup truck. Points at the license plate: XL IXRS. Asks me if I know what it means. It takes me less than a second to decode it— *49ers*—but my brain can't make sense of what is going on here. *Twofer?* It was the first time I'd heard the term. *Test?*

Izzy slaps Jack on the shoulder and scolds him, but he just guffaws again, bending over with his hands on his knees at the hilarity of it all. I can tell I am the butt of his joke but I still do not know why. It seems like a routine Izzy is used to.

For a second or two I stand there in the parking lot watching Jack laugh. Then I think maybe if I laugh too we'll all be in on the joke together. So I laugh, the moment passes, and I feel relief. But I am still confused.

When Jack finally quiets down I turn to Izzy. "Twofer?" She looks at me with a lopsided smile. "Oh, you know. Because you're Black *and* female. He's just being stupid." She holds her hands up as if to say *What can you do?* Then she turns away from the pickup truck and walks back toward our office. She does not wait for me to join her. I follow.

I feel like an idiot and so damn *naïve* for not seeing the naked truth of it in the first place. So is this the law school version of the comment Harris's father made in my high school math class, implying I was stealing an admissions slot with my Blackness—and femaleness? Or is it like the lady at the Stanford Shopping Center who'd presumed that athleticism had gotten me into Stanford? My spidey sense is telling me this guy just might be a racist good old boy asshole. But I have a good deal of respect for judges and lawyers. My mind does not want to go there.

XXXVI.

By the end of the 1989–90 school year, a group of mixed-race students at Stanford had created a new student group, called Spectrum, owing perhaps to the consciousness raised at RA Training that prior fall. I heard from a friend at Harvard that students there had done the same thing, calling their group "Prism." The terms "multiracial" and "biracial" are starting to appear in the media. Nationally, policy makers begin to debate whether the U.S. census could allow people to check multiple race boxes to reflect a heritage of more than one race.

When I hear about these developments in racial classification, I know I've been waiting my whole life for a term like "biracial" or "multiracial" to define the otherwise out-of-bounds nature of my existence. I begin using the terms interchangeably to describe myself, and it feels nourishing, invigorating, like I've received a transplant to replace a diseased organ and have a new lease on life. Finally, checking a box doesn't mean ignoring my mother. Finally, I have a term to explain why I look and sound different from so many other Blacks without that term being derogatory, like "Oreo."

But at the start these new labels draw criticism from Black professors, policy makers, and intellectuals. I hear a Black pundit discuss this on a television news show one day. Blacks are the result of intermixture either in recent times or historically, he reminds his audience, and if mixed-race people identify as multiracial on government forms, the official count of Black people could diminish enough to pull governmental resources away from the Black community where they are much needed. Between the lines of his argument—conveyed with his facial expression, not his words—is the critique that mixed people are just using these labels to distance ourselves from the Black community, maybe to try to be "better" than Black.

Am I?

I don't care about the critique. I'm not thinking about government programs or the extent to which my personal decision might impact a bigger number of people or a more macro set of outcomes. I am desperate for belonging, and I find it with "biracial" and "multiracial."

It is a truth and it is a relief and it is *A Chosen Exile*, as Allyson Hobbs would title her book on the historical practice of passing. And as with those who passed out of Blackness into whiteness over the centuries prior, I would find that standing on the edge of Blackness where it bleeds lighter and lighter and ultimately starts to look like white came with both privilege and pain.

SELF-LOATHING

I.

What I now know to have been true of myself in my childhood and young adulthood:

1. I hated being Black.
2. I was afraid of Black people.
3. I tried to be what white people valued.

In June 1990, Dan knelt before me on a beach in Half Moon Bay, California, gave me a beautiful ring he'd designed, and asked me to marry him. Later that summer I joined his father's family on a weeklong trip to Harbour Island, one of their favorite vacation spots in the Bahamas. The eight of us stay in a high-end resort right on the beach and I am starting to feel less like a nervous girlfriend who has to work hard to please and more like one of the family.

Tentatively, I begin to let my hair down. I engage Dan's father in conversation about social and political issues—nervously, not because we are on different sides of the political spectrum (we aren't) but because he is a corporate lawyer—in fact, a Harvard Law grad. He makes a game of banter and reasoning. I want to be a player.

Dan and many of his relatives are avid scuba divers and want to get in plenty of dive time on Harbour Island. I'm not a strong swimmer and I've had a fear of fish since early childhood, so I don't want to be anywhere near that, not even to snorkel. Instead I wave good-bye to the divers and stay behind with Dan's stepmother, Judy, and stepsister, Emily, and read novels on the sandy beach in the full sun. When the divers return hours later, I get up to greet them, admiring my darkening skin as I walk toward them, tossing my curly twists of hair now rope-like from being air-dried in the salty Caribbean breeze.

The eight of us gather each night for dinner at a restaurant down the beach. Dan's father has a fabulous sense of humor and he reels off joke after hilarious joke as the tiki torches flicker in the darkening night and we sip drinks thick with rum. Some nights we play poker after dinner, a game my Daddy and brothers had taught me young, and I delight in showing this new family that I know a thing or two about the game. One night, we linger late into the evening, singing whichever songs any of us can think of, full-throated and with harmony.

I miss Dan when he dives. Twenty-nine years later we still don't enjoy being apart, but in those earliest days of togetherness I ached without him. Toward the end of our vacation, I ask if I can go out on the boat with them even if I don't dive. Dan's father says it is no problem.

He reserves time with the local dive master, and the next day, off we go, Dan, his father, his brother, his stepbrother, his stepbrother's friend, me, the dive master, the guy driving the boat, and a few strangers who also booked time on the boat. I am the only person of color. And boy am I. After five days in the strong sun I am a rich chocolate brown.

We board the small boat and spend the thirty-minute ride across the water chitchatting. As we bump along the waves Dan's father tells some fabulous jokes and we all laugh. When the dive master finds the right spot, the boatman slows and then anchors the boat, and the divers shift into gear. It is all de rigueur for these seasoned divers, but between the complicated equipment and the overarching safety issues I don't want to be in the way. So I scoot toward the back corner of the boat to witness their rituals. One by one each diver sits on the edge of the boat and does a backward roll off the side. I yell a good-bye to each. When it is Dan's turn to roll off, he comes over to me and gives me a kiss. Then it's just me and the boatman—a weathered-looking white man. I make small talk with him for a bit and then take a novel out of my bag, pull a hat over my eyes, stretch out my legs, and begin reading.

Forty-five minutes later all of the divers are back, regaling me and each other with stories about what they'd experienced. One had huffed and puffed too much and had had to come up quickly. One had seen a shark. One had gone farther down than he'd ever gone before. I listen intently and ask questions. The trip back is quieter than the trip out, the divers spent. Dan puts his arm around me and I lay my head against his shoulder. Before I know it we are back at the dock.

We gather our things and one by one step onto the dock. The dive master and boatman are huddled in conversation apparently over some paperwork. I am the last to get off, and as I stand on the ledge of the unsteady boat and step tentatively onto the dock, the boatman grabs me hard by the shoulder, his hand like a pincer.

"Wait, you. What do you think you're up to? You didn't pay."

They seem to think I am a freeloader. An urchin who'd just clung to this opportunity for a boat ride. *Hadn't they seen me with my family? Hadn't they listened? Hadn't they seen Dan's tenderness toward me?*

"What? I, I—I'm with them," I stammer, nodding toward Dan and his family who are trudging away from me toward the boathouse where they'll return their equipment. The boatman still has me by the shoulder. As he shakes me, the diamond on my engagement ring sparkles in the intense Caribbean sun. "I'm his fiancée," I stammer, pointing to my hand and jerking my chin toward my family.

I finally shout for Dan. He is now about twenty feet away and he turns around and looks confused to find that I am not right there behind him. Dan's father hears the commotion and turns to look, too. "He won't . . . he doesn't," I stammer, waving my hands in small circles, still in the clutch of the boatman's gnarled hand. "He says I didn't pay!"

"She's with us," Dan's father shouts and makes a broad sweep of his hands. The boatman releases me. Dan's father turns and keeps walking.

I am shaking. Dan runs toward me. He looks to the boatman and at me and then back at the boatman, asking with his eyes what is going on, silently demanding an explanation or apology. But both the boatman and the dive master turn away and busy themselves with something on the boat. I grab Dan's hand and step off the boat and I do not look back at the men.

We walk toward the resort hand in hand. I try to explain what had happened, but there is nothing in Dan's life that makes any of this make sense to him.

That night I slept fitfully. They'd treated me like a stowaway. Like a freed Black with no papers. Being some white man's property is what actually spared me from whatever might have happened. Escape and a cage all at once.

III.

After dating almost exclusively white boys all my life, at age twenty-four I marry Dan in a small ceremony in a mansion on the eastern bank of the Hudson River near West Point, about two hours north of Snedens Landing where I'd lived as a small child. In preparation for the wedding, I go to a Black hair salon for the second time in my life—this time on my own terms. Instead of leaving with the short Afro Angie and my mother had conspired to give me in the sixth grade, I emerge with extensions woven into my hair—dark brown tresses made of real human hair that flow long, thick, and supple, which I can flick and let fall or tuck behind my ear. This time I look like any Black girl who knows how to make her hair look the way it is supposed to. Who knows how to make her hair look beautiful.

White hair. White dress. White life.

IV.

In December of my second year of law school, Dan and I want to celebrate his birthday by going out to dinner in Boston's North End. It is 1992. We wedge our car into a parking spot on a narrow street a few blocks away from the restaurant and walk down the sidewalk hand in hand feeling the brisk chill as dusk falls on the night. I'm a little nervous walking these streets. While my law school is located in Cambridge, a cosmopolitan city with people from all over the world, Boston is known as a balkanized city with pockets of deeply embedded racism. We are an interracial couple in the wrong part of town lured by the promise of great Italian food.

On the opposite side of the narrow street, maybe thirty feet or so in front of us, a man walks toward us. As we near him I see him do a double take, which I take as a kind gesture so I return his gaze, begin to smile, and prepare to nod. But he stares back at me with no smile as if he is studying us. I look straight ahead and keep walking and then I look back over at the man, hoping to see we are of no interest to him. But the man is now almost even with us and he is staring straight at me. He passes under a streetlight. I see pale skin, squinted eyes, and an upper lip starting to tremble like the mouth of a growling dog.

I could be wrong. This could be all kinds of things. He could be deranged. Could be mad at something else. Could want to harm us for reasons having nothing to do with race. I just know I need to get out of there.

I squeeze Dan's hand tight and mutter *walk faster baby we need to walk faster* as I quicken my pace and Dan has no choice but to follow. After twenty brisk paces we round the corner and I turn around and peek in the direction from which we'd just come. The man is walking off into the night.

"What?" Dan asks. "Why did you speed up like that? What were you saying?" He hadn't noticed. Never had to notice. Had not learned to notice.

V.

In 1993 I am a summer associate at the Palo Alto office of the law firm Cooley Godward in what is, at the time, the firm's largest-ever class of summer recruits. Thirty-one law students, each with uncreased briefcases and brand-new suits, jockey to prove our mettle to the partners and to discover the pecking order among ourselves. I am determined to be one of the best.

The only Black partner in the three-hundred-lawyer firm is Tom Jackson. A six-foot-six guy with dark skin, a long stride, and a personality that is alternately captivating and terrifying. You love his hearty chortle unless he is actually laughing *at* you, which is always a distinct possibility. No one is immune.

He'll come out of his huge corner office and stand near his secretary's carrel and begin to tell a story in a voice loud enough for anyone within forty feet to hear. Lawyers of various ages, and in particular we young ones, come out from behind our desks and stand in our doorways listening, hanging on every word. A fellow summer associate has the great misfortune of having a name one letter off from Tom's—Tom Jackston—and one day the summer associate's biweekly paycheck accidentally gets delivered to Tom the partner. He stands at his secretary's carrel opening his mail and comes upon the paycheck and shouts, "What is this shit?" Then he strides down the hall to the other Tom's office and throws the paycheck at him, laughing that it isn't enough to cover more than a pair of new shoes.

Whenever I hear Tom's heavy footsteps coming down the hall toward my office, my heart starts beating wildly. One day he shows up at my door.

"You busy?" It is more of a bark than a question.
"Um, no?"
"Great. You're coming with me."

He turns around and walks away. I scurry out from behind my desk, grab my briefcase, and race after Tom, who is striding toward the elevators. I catch up to him and we stand waiting in silence. I fidget with the buttons on my double-breasted navy blazer. I am dying to know where we are going—and for how long—but don't dare ask.

We get to his Lexus sport coupe. He opens the passenger door for me. I sit down and he shuts the door and walks around to the other side. I tuck my briefcase in the footwell and begin smoothing my long navy-and-white-striped skirt. "So where are we going?" I finally ask as he eases the car out of the parking lot and onto the main road. "You'll see." I try to affect casual, as if I don't care that I have no idea what is going on. I try, even, to be delighted by it.

When I cross my right leg over my left and settle back into the bucket seat, I notice my right shoe. It is black. But I was sure I was wearing my navy pumps! I uncross my legs and stare at both feet now side by side in the footwell. One is navy and one is black. As I'd soon learn, Tom and I are headed to court for a hearing. Tom is mentoring me and all I have to do is pay attention. But all I can think about is the ribbing I'll get if Tom notices my shoes.

Toward the end of the summer, a huge complaint comes in and it becomes my job to analyze and dismiss every case cited by the other side. I stay at the office until midnight or one a.m. every day for a week. When the memo is done, I leave it on Tom's chair and creep home in the dark of night. The next day I'm in line for lunch at the little café in our office complex. Tom comes up behind me and my heart starts to pound. "That was one helluva memo, kid." That's all he says. It was all he needed to say. I am making it even in this Black partner's eyes. I know he's been counting on me to get this right.

VI.

In spring of my third year of law school I am in Professor Charles Ogletree's coveted criminal justice clinic where, per Massachusetts law, as a third-year law student I can represent defendants in low-level hearings. My clients are battered women and juveniles. "Tree," as we call him, is one of a handful of Blacks on the faculty and I and other students of color gravitate to his warm, intentional mentoring.

I am also working on my thesis—a requirement to graduate—under the direction of Professor Martha Minow, a white woman and an expert in family law who years later will become the school's dean. It is 1994. I choose to write on the particular injustice mixed-race kids face when it comes to moving from foster care to adoptive homes. I argue that transracial adoption is inherently better than the foster care system, which as a rule urges parents *not* to bond with their foster child. That a permanent, loving, adoptive home of *any* race is better than the foster care system.

This is the same general topic I'd argued in Steyer's civil rights seminar back in college, but now I have a new weapon in my arsenal—the new labels "multiracial" and "biracial" that are gaining traction among federal and state policy makers. Armed with the new race classification schema I argue that the government has no business deciding which aspect of a multiracial/biracial child's heritage gets preference in adoption placement. As I'd done with the *Drummond* case back in college, I dismiss the importance of "cultural heritage transmission" for Black kids as pseudoscience. I argue that by keeping mixed-race kids in foster care longer than white kids until a suitable Black adoptive family can be found, the government is denying those mixed kids the equal protection of the law on the basis of their race.

My feeling—based on my own lived experience—was that white parents could raise Black babies just fine. After all, I was raised in a white community largely by my white mother and *I was fine.* Mom was the one who told the Mormon missionaries at our door that they had nothing to offer us because "we are a Black family." I'd made it up and out of childhood to college and now to graduate school and I knew I hadn't had as much as one drop of this "cultural transmission." And *I was fine.*

I wrote that thesis furiously, arguing specifically that it wasn't the government's right to call mixed-race kids "Black" and subject them to these "cultural transmission" rituals, which sounded almost like voodoo to me. The counterargument—that mixed kids raised by white parents were *not fine*—was a mirror too closely held up to my own face. I had to look away.

VII.

That May, my brother Stephen died at age forty-three after a short but intense bout with pneumonia. He'd spent his entire career as a public interest lawyer in Chicago, and when he died was the Vice President of the ACLU of Illinois.

He was the brother I knew best of all my big siblings because he was the last to leave Nigeria for college, and had gone to law school in Wisconsin when Daddy, Mom, and I lived there. He'd been the one to take me to the Jack and Jill cotillion at the end of high school. He was the brother who'd cautioned me against writing my law school application personal statement about my dawning racial consciousness because it might be interpreted the wrong way. He was a confidant of things I wasn't even intending to share. And he loved me anyway.

At Christmas five months before his death, Stephen had given all of us Lythcotts a strange and weighty gift—a printout of the genealogical research he'd done on our family. This was before the Internet could tell you these things with the press of a few buttons. Stephen had walked and talked his way through courthouses and graveyards toward this understanding of our slave ancestor Silvey and her descendants, and had begun to fashion a narrative out of it. A story.

Through Stephen's work I now knew I was a seventh-generation American, descended from folks long buried in unheralded plots in and around Charleston, South Carolina. Thanks to the painstaking work of my beautiful dead brother, I would one day come to know I was Silvey's child. But at the time he gave me this gift I was not interested in the relic of ancestry.

VIII.

One month after Stephen died I graduate from law school. I'd had to slap blinders on my eyes, on my heart, to get from his funeral to my thesis and through final exams. Next up is the bar exam, which I'll take in July.

I'd accepted a job offer with Cooley Godward, which meant I'd be starting my law career in California and would therefore have to take the California Bar Exam, which vies with New York's for the title of being the most difficult to pass. Many people retake it. Many times. To have any chance at passing this three-day exam, you had to study like hell for eight weeks straight.

I was adamant about passing on the first try. The lawyers at Cooley Godward were counting on me to pass. I wasn't going to be that Black person who didn't pass the first time.

Bar study begins a week before graduation. I set up a grid of how many hours I have to study each day and which topics I need to cover. I need no distractions for these eight weeks, including the regular hassle of caring for my impossible hair. So for the third time in my twenty-six years I take myself off to a Black hair salon and for the first time I ask for a real Black hairstyle: braids. Seven hours and $200 later I have them, a gleaming set of thin long ropes that spring out from my scalp like a dome. I shake my head from side to side, enjoying the swish they make against my shoulders and the way they look the same whether I swing them to the left or the right or catch a glimpse of them from the back. Gone are the frizzy bits, the untamable sections. My new braids are as beautiful as they are expensive, and yes, as I'd hoped, they are very simple to care for.

What I hadn't counted on was how differently I'd be treated with these braids. I take the same bus and subway lines to and from my apartment on Massachusetts Avenue in Cambridge. Go to the same grocery store and restaurants. But some white strangers now glance warily at me on the sidewalk, pull their bodies and arms away from me and into themselves as I walk past. At the Star Market a white mother looks over at me and then puts a protective arm around her child while keeping her eyes on me.

It is wild. Like taking a high-power microscope to racism and seeing it writhe and wriggle under the glaring light. And it is depressing.

I know from experience and academic study of these issues that one's life—*my* life—as a light-skinned biracial Black person is one of relative racial privilege. My skin that in winter wanes from brown paper bag to high yellow and my so-called white way of talking assuages whites who might otherwise have been fearful of me. Seven hours spent getting braids in a Black salon somehow overrides this, and catapults me onto a higher level on the Blackness spectrum. At least in the eyes of some whites in Cambridge, Massachusetts.

For years I'd been trying to be more Black to fit with Black people while simultaneously trying to pass as white enough to avoid the judgment of whites. But these braids are making me seem more Black to *whites*— which I'd never known was my goal; only in the experience of it do I begin to understand how important this is to me.

I know for the first time that I'd craved to be Black in the eyes of whites. I'd never belonged with or to whites, so being seen as Black by whites was a way to definitively belong *somewhere* to *something* and *someone*, even while my actual relationship to the Black community was still tenuous. In this sense my braids feel like an upgrade. A promotion. An invitation past the bouncer into the club. My braids actively do away with the ambiguity I'd struggled with for most of my conscious life. They look white people in the eye and say, "Yes I'm Black" in ways my own vocal cords and life experience have never articulated. Until sporting the braids, I'd been drawn in pencil. Smudge-able. Erasable. With the braids I am redrawn in ink.

I cherish them for four months through studying for the Bar Exam and a few months beyond, but next up is a law firm in Silicon Valley where Black hair is considered unkempt even in a place boasting "casual Friday" dress. I remove the braids myself and go back to blowing my hair dry and smoothing it straight with an iron.

When I take the braids out, my identity's temporarily strong outline begins to fade. I move west, start work at Cooley, and right before Thanksgiving I learn that I passed the California Bar Exam on the first try.

IX.

I'd wanted to become a lawyer so I could help the underdog. In college, classmates had pinned posters of celebrity crushes to their dorm room walls, and I'd taped up a picture of Thurgood Marshall, who'd argued for the desegregation of American public schools before the Supreme Court and won, and who later served as our nation's first Black Supreme Court Justice. I believed in law as the tool that could help Blacks and people of color more broadly, and all of those who are culturally and systematically disregarded in America. In law school, I'd joined the *Civil Rights–Civil Liberties Law Review*, and I'd found a public interest faculty mentor in Charles Ogletree.

But when early in my third year my classmates and I were trying to land permanent jobs to start the year following, I couldn't shake the psychological pressure I felt from the law school community suggesting that corporate jobs were most prestigious and therefore most desirable and therefore necessary for someone who looked like me, someone who might want to demonstrate to the world that I was impressive and worthy. I was a middle-of-the-pack student in law school, which made me feel ashamed, and I worried that if I took a public interest job people would think I hadn't been able to land an offer from a prominent law firm. (In reality, the best public interest jobs are just as selective as the firms, if not more so.)

I ignored the personal values that had drawn me to law school and had guided my curricular choices and took a corporate job with Cooley instead. I told myself that because I'd taken out loans to finance my tuition, room, and board, I couldn't *afford* to go the public interest route, but that was a naked lie. Harvard had a loan repayment program explicitly for those who went into public interest law.

I'd gone to law school to help other people but I took a corporate job to help myself.

X.

It is 1994. I am an intellectual property litigator in Silicon Valley specializing in trademarks at the birth of the commercialized Internet. Netscape goes public in the summer of 1995 and heralds the start of the dot-com era. I am very well paid, well regarded, and being groomed for greater opportunities. There is just one problem; the work is sucking the life out of me one billable hour at a time.

I thought I'd done everything right.

XI.

Late summer 1995. I am twenty-seven. Dan and I are in our third year as a married couple and we rent a tiny house in Silicon Valley. For the past few months a tightening feeling had formed in my stomach every Sunday afternoon as I thought about going into work at the firm the next day. Dan, who was working at an exhibit design firm, was also feeling unhappy in his career.

One weekend evening, he and I sit on the concrete slab back porch of our house and talk. I thought I'd known what I wanted to do with my life, thought I'd charted the right path, but I am far afield from the way I had hoped to feel about my life. I say all of this through scads of tears, blowing my snotty nose, sitting amid mounting piles of tissue.

Then I give myself a talking-to.

You of all people have no right to be miserable you with an upper-middle-class childhood you with loving parents and a great education and all of that does not equal miserable so stop your pathetic crying and get your shit together.

I want to help humans. This I know. I need to work for an organization that helps humans. I think of the law-based public interest organizations I admired—ACLU, Legal Aid—that I fear will now see me as a sellout and reject any effort I might make to join them. I think of how, while I had loved the oral argument of the mock litigation in college and law school, I am growing to despise the actual red tape of litigation, the hoops one has to jump through, the posturing one has to do just to get a case started, the slim chance of any of it ever being heard by a judge. A wistfulness had begun to stir in me as I drove past the Stanford campus while traveling to and from work each day. I can picture the faces of the people who'd believed in me when I was struggling in college. I want to be part of the effort to help young people find their footing and craft a meaningful life. I think maybe I should do admissions work or student affairs.

I begin applying for those kinds of jobs.

XII.

In October of 1995, almost one year to the day after I joined Cooley Godward, Daddy dies. He'd had prostate cancer for years, had felt it coming, and had chosen to die from it. He was seventy-seven and had already exceeded the life expectation for a Black man in America. He knew something would get him, and prostate cancer was it. He died in the house my parents had chosen to be their final home together: a few acres in the woods on Martha's Vineyard off the coast of Massachusetts. There'd been enough time for us all to get there to say good-bye.

After Daddy died I take three weeks off work to help my Mom with the logistics of insurance and banking and bills. I don't ask the firm for permission to stay so long, really. I just stay with my Mom until I feel she can start to walk through her days alone. When I return to work in November, I muddle through the interminably long days and stumble through cloudy thinking. I can't make a to-do list. Can't follow it when I do manage to make one. The holidays come and go. My billable hours dip significantly.

Three months after Daddy died, I confide in my sister-in-law, Stephen's widow, about my inability to get anything done. She encourages me to go to grief counseling. I haven't had so much as an hour of therapy in my life and tend to dismiss it as a crutch for the weak, but I go, if only to make my sister-in-law feel she is helping me.

After just one session with a group of fellow grievers, counseling becomes a biweekly lifeline. There, I begin to talk about my brother's unexpected death as well as Daddy's. For seven months, until the funk dissipates and I begin to feel like my old self again, those twice-monthly group sessions are my religion.

Sometime during those months of therapy, the partner with whom I worked most closely takes me out to lunch, a rare treat. We walk to the restaurant, have a nice meal, and then as we are walking back to the firm she stops on the sidewalk. Turns to me.

"You need to get your hours up."
"I know. It's been hard for me since my dad died."
"I understand. I know what it's like. I lost both my parents when I was young. You work through it, you move on."
"I know. I'm actually in counseling."
"Good. But you need to get your hours up."

XIII.

I go for those student affairs and admissions jobs at Stanford three times over two years and three times I am rejected either for lacking the requisite experience or for being viewed as overqualified given my law degree and experience as a lawyer. With each rejection I feel that an escape hatch has been shut in my face.

XIV.

In the spring of 1996, Dan and I attend his cousin's wedding in the Florida Keys. The rehearsal dinner is at a restaurant with lovely views of the ocean and Dan and I walk down the boardwalk toward it hand in hand. We pass people at outdoor restaurants drinking and laughing in their tropical shirts and white pants. A white man seated at a corner table catches sight of us and begins to stare. I squeeze Dan's hand tight, which is now my cue to him that something is going on. Dan looks in the direction of my gaze and sees it too. We keep walking ahead with purposeful confidence, though feigned. I look back once and see the man continuing to stare at us as we walk.

Dan had learned about the white racist sneer. Life with me was beginning to teach him.

XV.

I take on more pro bono work at the law firm as a way to make my corporate law practice resemble in some small way the reason I'd gotten a law degree in the first place. One case is a huge death penalty appeal with a dozen other lawyers. Another is small—a Black male child is incarcerated at the California Youth Authority for having punched a white child and I am to be his lawyer. It is the middle of 1997.

My mentor for this pro bono litigation work is an acerbic white female litigator at my firm. She is a very busy senior associate and makes it clear that she has little time for me. Frankly I am a little afraid of her so I am happy enough getting to do this on my own. I drive out to Stockton where my client is being held and I interview him. I stay late for many nights to prepare to conduct my first-ever deposition—a deposition of the school administrator who'd broken up the fight between my client and the other child. The week of the deposition I pass my mentor in the hallway. She barks at me. "Ready for that depo?" Yes, I assure her.

The day came. My mentor and I, opposing counsel, the court reporter, and the person being deposed gather in the conference room for the depo. I begin with the opening procedural ritual. I speak nervously. Tentatively. My mentor begins to fidget in her chair. Then she speaks.

"No. No. Are you kidding me? Wait, just—no."

Opposing counsel looks at me with sympathy. Sweat sprouts on my forehead and upper lip. I had spoken all of a dozen words so far. *Am I that bad that she needs to be interrupting me like this?* The walls of the conference room feel like they are pressing in on me. Blood pounds in my veins.

My mentor speaks to the room. "We're going to postpone." Humiliated, I shake my head and stare at my pile of papers, then gather my things and get the hell out of there. I walk back to my office berating myself for not having practiced more, for not observing more people do a depo, for being so incompetent at the task of trying to stand up for this Black child. But the senior associate had given me all of ninety seconds. I might have gotten into the swing of it if I'd just been given a bit more of a chance.

I left the firm for good a few months later to take a position in the trademarks division at Intel's legal department.

Someone else took over the case. I don't know what happened to this child. But I will never forget his name.

XVI.

A year into my work as a trademark lawyer at Intel, a friend who works as the Dean of Students at Stanford Law School calls to tell me she is going on maternity leave and do I want to try to cover her job for three months? I tell my manager at Intel that I might not want to be a lawyer anymore. That I might want to work in student affairs. She says she values me and agrees to hold my job. "For your sake I hope you love it. For my sake I hope you don't."

Mere days into the job I know I love the work, which boils down to giving a damn about these law students and supporting them as they encounter obstacles in their academic or personal life. I feel like I have my self back. The only gnawing fear is how I will stomach returning to corporate law when the maternity leave ends.

In January of 1999, my friend tells the law school dean that she is not going to return from maternity leave. The dean calls me to say he wants to hire me permanently. And after two and a half years of trying to conceive a child, where sex has felt less like pleasure and more like a physical therapy regime, I am now finally pregnant myself.

XVII.

I am thriving. What I enjoy most about this new work is supporting students of color and students from other underrepresented communities in keeping their nose to the grindstone and their eyes on the prize when life tries to get in the way. I am making less money than I'd made as a lawyer, and the trajectory for future income is nowhere near as high as that of a lawyer, but the knot in my stomach as I think about going to work the next day is gone. And that is worth its weight in gold.

I feel engaged and productive as a problem solver in the lives of humans. We have a little baby boom in the student population with five or six students who themselves are pregnant or whose partners are, and it seems only logical to take an unused storage closet and spruce it up and outfit it to serve as a room for nursing mothers. I also have a fantastic boss and mentor in Paul Brest, an exalted white male law professor who engages me in conversation as if my mind works well and my thoughts genuinely interest him. As if we are equals in the work of helping other humans thrive.

Now in a more relaxed and welcoming work environment, now enjoying myself in my career, now surrounded by many more people of color in the law school student body, and on the faculty and staff, I stop pressing my hair flat and pulling it into a ponytail or bun and begin to let my hair down. Wear it natural. I experiment with the creams and conditioners made for hair like mine that are being developed in response to a burgeoning population of mixed race women, and that I can find via the Internet.

In May of 1999 when I am thick with nine months of pregnancy, waddling up and down stairs, just hoping my water won't break until the school term is over, one of our students takes his life. I'd interacted with him a number of times. He was tall and thin, sweet and funny, and had eyes that shone with curiosity and intellect. Whenever he showed up at my door I knew he'd be warm and respectful, and present a problem he'd already gone to great lengths to resolve before coming to me.

The day after his death his shattered parents come to Paul's office late in the afternoon, and Paul asks me and a few other university officials to be there with him. Together we sit with the parents as disbelief gives way to frustration and when, finally, their anguish releases. We know we'd perhaps known their son in ways they did not, and know just as equally that none of that is relevant now.

The conversation ebbs and flows from the sadness to the practicalities of the young man's belongings, records, and so forth, back to the emotional, and even the existential. Seeing the meeting going long into the night, Paul nudges, then urges, then with his eyes almost begs me to go home. I sit on his couch with my legs neatly tucked beneath me, wearing the black maternity dress I'd put on that morning after hearing the news. I just smile gently at Paul and nod a silent *thanks but I'm okay.*

Later in trying to be more aware of why exactly I loved the work I was now doing, I'd reflect back on this night sitting with parents experiencing the first shock waves of the unimaginable, and I'd see it clearly. The law partner who'd taken me to lunch implored me to work longer hours despite my grief; here, in total contrast, amid the greatest crisis a school administration can experience, was a boss telling me to go take care of myself. I learned that night that bearing witness to the suffering of another human is the most sacred work we can do.

XVIII.

In June of 1999 my baby boy is born.

We name him Sawyer.

When he gets to be about two, people begin asking him his name instead of directing that question to Dan or me. He is eager to reply.

"August."
"No, not when were you *born* but what's your *name*."
"I was born in June. My name is Sawyer. But I wish my parents had called me August."

Sawyer learned to talk in full sentences before he could walk. So these conversations would set strangers back a bit, not only for the logic of it all but for the quality of this tiny person's language.

"August" had been on the short list of names we'd considered, and we'd told him so. I'd loved the name three times over: for its homage to the Black playwright August Wilson, for being the month in which Dan and I were married; for being an adjective I'd hoped would indeed describe my son when he was a grown man one day. But we didn't want people to reduce this magnificent name to Gus or Augie, which we'd also told him. Unwittingly we'd given our son a name shared by fiction's most mischievous white boy. It would be years before I'd be a person who'd lament the lost opportunity to name him after a Black man.

XIX.

Sawyer was beautiful from the first moment I saw him, pale with the slick straight jet black hair of a newborn. In a few months his skin tone became a medium brown and his hair began to grow in medium brown as well with the loop and curl of Blackness. And he was born to a mother who would wear her hair natural from then on.

XX.

After trying for more than two years to conceive Sawyer, my body seemed to have figured out how to be pregnant; in October of 2000, just weeks after starting a new position with Stanford's incoming president, John Hennessy, I got pregnant again without even trying. I wouldn't discover I was pregnant until severe morning sickness began to consume me in December. My daughter, Avery, was born in 2001, six weeks before 9/11.

When we brought Avery home from the hospital, Sawyer—just shy of two years and two months old—looked over at me and said, "For ages, and ages, and ages, and ages I've wanted a baby sister." He bonded with her from the start and she received and returned that love like a reflex. Sixteen years later, they are bonded still.

Having grown up lonely as the only child of my parents, the only young child in an extended family of much older half siblings, the only child on this strange interracial island, witnessing an unyielding bond between my children gives me such hope that if all else fails they will have each other.

XXI.

When I learn I am pregnant with a girl, I feel almost giddy at the thought
of teaching her what no one taught me about Black hair:

1. Never take a brush to it.
2. Don't shampoo too often.
3. Condition condition condition.
4. Wet it, and rake through it with fingers or a wide-toothed comb.
5. Use leave-in conditioner to bring out smooth ringlets.
6. Once set, don't you dare touch it until it dries.

I will not let you look like a tumbleweed.
I will not let your hair pouf in humid air.
I will not give you a hairstyle high school boys will tease.
I will buy every single product you need.
It will be my job—my *joy*—to help you achieve the self-acceptance that
eluded me until midlife.

I vow to my unborn daughter: *Baby, your mother will get it right.*

XXII.

I do not resemble my mother and so? I am desperate for my daughter
to resemble me. Like her brother, my girl is a beautiful newborn with
pale skin and shiny wet jet-black hair. In the first months of her life, her
hair grows in brown and curly too. Unlike her brother though, when
her skin begins to darken it seems to pause midway. It is just a pause,
I am sure.

Her darkness is coming.

I am sure.

I am wrong.

XXIII.

In occasional quiet moments when my baby girl is asleep in my arms, I gaze down at her and my mind retreats to its dark corner where the most frightening questions hide. *She's so light. Am I sure she is mine?*

Yes, I have proof, my mind reminds me. When Dan first brought her to me minutes after the Cesarean section, she was swaddled and still a bit wet, and as I gazed upon this lovely little face I noticed a tiny cut of no more than half a centimeter above her left eyebrow, a cut that was still there when we brought her home from the hospital five days later. Thanks to my ob-gyn's careless nick of an otherwise flawless, perfect newborn, I can be certain this girl in my arms is mine.

And there is the matter of her white Daddy. Whom I chose.
Yes, I chose him.

XXIV.

In 2002, when Avery is one and Sawyer is three, I launch a new office on campus and hold a newly created position: dean of freshmen. My job will be to try to build a sense of belonging in our undergraduates, to benefit the students in the immediate term and the university over the long haul. Research shows that students thrive when they feel a sense of belonging, and they feel a sense of belonging if one faculty member or staff person takes an interest in them. My new office will try to increase the likelihood of that happening for all students from the get-go.

I hold this role until 2012. It is joyful work almost every single day. What I love most is showing first-generation students, poor students, students of color, queer students, and anyone who grew up feeling like "the other" that I believe in them, and by extension the university believes in them, even when under the crushing weight of stereotype they don't believe in themselves.

XXV.

By the time Avery is two her skin holds a tint of tan so subtle you might mistake it for sun exposure, while Sawyer, now four, looks much more like me. Avery's soft, curly locks have given way to the wavy, tangle-free stuff of a new Barbie doll, neither too thin nor too thick, almost synthetically sleek. She gets frustrated because it won't hold a braid without a hair tie, and barrettes won't stay in place; mine, on the other hand, ties itself in knots that only certain products, not available at white markets, can untangle.

I sit behind her at the dresser, as my mother did with me, staring at us both in the mirror, as my mother did with me. Slowly I brush through her long brown hair, thinking *I'm glad for her that she has what we call good hair. I'm glad she'll have an easy time.* But I end every brushstroke with a twirl of the lock around my index finger, trying to tease out a ringlet or two, trying to force a resemblance to me. Trying to bring out the Black.

White parents slather their kids with sunblock, but it isn't cancer I worry about. I hold Avery up to the strong California sun. *Darken her. Make her mine.*

How will she identify?
How will others see her?
Will she feel the swift kick in the gut when someone says the N-word?
Will she stand up for me?

I brace for some white person to ask if I am her nanny.

XXVI.

When Sawyer and Avery are still quite young I begin my new and improved version of my parents' political advocacy campaign ("You are Black!"):

> You are part Black, Eastern European Jew, and Yorkshire coal miner.

> Your ancestors were some of the most reviled people in history.

> Be proud of that and of them.

> You have the right to be here.

> You come from people who survived.

I try to say it not as declaration or dare—as my parents' line had sometimes felt to me—but as support, as a kind of reassurance that might become a part of the structure of their developing minds, as ballast when the destabilization comes at them from wherever it might come.

XXVII.

I hold a position among the senior ranks of the Stanford administration: assistant vice provost for undergraduate education and dean of freshmen. Two years into this brand-new role I begin hearing from parents, students, alumni, and colleagues that my new role is making a difference. I am well paid. And my natural, springy coils are part and parcel of my persona. But there is a lingering shadow. A cloak laid across my shoulders I can't seem to shake.

In the outside world my title raises smiling eyebrows and praise. Within academe—not just at Stanford but nationally—the hierarchy of graduate degrees says the PhD is supreme, says that those who went to graduate school to study law, medicine, or business are more doers than thinkers. Beneath the surface of that widely held opinion lies the bias that those without PhDs are not as intelligent as those who have them. It's a bias we can ignore, work hard to contradict, or let eat away at us.

The vice provost to whom I report at Stanford is a PhD-clad faculty member from engineering. When he is considering me as a possibility for the newly vacated role as head of the undergraduate advising office, he runs through the qualifications like a cross-examination.

"You have a JD, right?"
"Right."
"From Harvard."
"Right."
"Okay, good."

This was 2004. I didn't get the promotion then. I would get it in 2009.

In the meantime, the three others who reported to this vice provost— all women, all white, all at least ten years older than I was—had PhDs. At our staff meetings I at times struggle to make myself heard, feel they are overlooking my perspective, feel desperate, even, to make my ideas count as I put forth idea after idea about how to improve the freshman experience from my vantage point as the university's first freshman dean. Occasionally I feel almost paranoid about being excluded from important conversations. Even cloaked in a degree from Harvard Law School, it seems I might not be good enough.

Is it the wrong degree or the wrong skin color? Is my Blackness so Black that it trumps the bona fides of Harvard? Am I less smart? Am I less smart because of my brain or my Blackness? Do I have to be more smart to be considered just as good? Is all of this happening in their eyes or only in mine?

Years later I'd learn I'd not been paranoid.

XXVIII.

In 2004 we created a new freshman orientation program at Stanford called "Three Books," our take on the common book experience most colleges and universities provide for new students. Our program would feature not one but three texts which would be assigned to the students to read over the summer, and the program would culminate in the three authors coming to campus all at once to participate in a moderated conversation about their books and their lives as writers.

A group of us—one faculty member and the rest staff—develop the concept and when the first incarnation is over and done with in September of 2004, we begin brainstorming texts for 2005. The faculty member urges us to consider *Possession* by A. S. Byatt, so I buy it and begin reading it. But rather quickly, as if meeting a closed door suddenly on my path, I am struck that this text will be a barrier to the many incoming students who had not been exposed to complex works of metafiction in high school. I page through Byatt recalling myself as a seventeen-year-old, who'd been plucked from the relative mediocrity of my Midwestern public high school and had suddenly to confront texts of immense complexity in college. With Byatt in my hands I was seventeen again, trying to immerse myself in the book I'd been assigned as an incoming freshman—*The Name of the Rose*, by Umberto Eco—a novel I'd struggled to comprehend day after late summer day in Wisconsin back in 1985. I recalled the shame I felt in the Branner lounge as Kennell discussed it with us, at barely being able to read Eco for comprehension let alone mastery. I'd felt marginalized just when the next important chapter of my life was opening in front of me.

As dean I know that many of our incoming students—those who were tops in their high school but whose high school was not relatively rigorous—would feel admitted but not let in to the club of thinkers at Stanford if we slammed Byatt on them as part of New Student Orientation. I had been that kid and I am doing this work in no small part to care about those kids and help pave the way for their ultimate success. Let them become exposed to those texts in the weeks and months to come under the guidance of professors and other instructors, I tell my colleagues. What they need to feel most is a sense of belonging at the start; let's not make them feel excluded. As I sit around our conference room table making this argument on behalf of the next generation of kids, I am aware that I am outing myself as someone who had once struggled with the assigned freshman text. Peeling back this layer of armor, I feel naked. Maybe I am.

XXIX.

I fill Avery's bedroom with stuffed animals as well as Black dolls, like the dolls my mother gave me—alternatives to the definitive white blonde blue-eyed ideal of beauty all around. Psychologists say Black dolls are important for enhancing a Black child's self-esteem.

Or will she have white self-esteem?

I give my daughter these dolls, hold her to the sun, tease a curl around my finger, and talk to her about Silvey.

It is lonely on my island and I want to bring my Avery to me there.

XXX.

On August 29, 2005, Katrina makes landfall and the levees do not hold as the Army knew they would not and the water sweeps life out from under the living.

In New Orleans's Ninth Ward, Black people on rooftops wave signs hastily scrawled on pieces of cardboard: "Help us." The people plead with their bodies and their signs, sure as the helicopters fly over that their government is coming for them. Will help them.

Instead the government flies by.

Over thirty thousand residents stream into the Louisiana Superdome, a building whose roof would leak, whose air-conditioning and refrigeration would fail, where, without enough food, water, restrooms, or restroom supplies, these residents would live for five days. As the Superdome grows more dank with a stench that is a mixture of rotting food, urine, and feces, the government relocates people to the Astrodome, over 350 miles away from their homes, in Houston. The Astrodome and the organizational wherewithal of Houston's local government save the day and save lives. Some evacuees will stay for weeks, some for months.

The former First Lady of the United States, Barbara Bush, takes a tour of the Astrodome on September 5, 2005, when it is brand-new in its role as savior. She chortles, "So many of the people in the arena here, you know, were underprivileged anyway, so this is working very well for them."

Most of us Black folks are Democrats. We believe as Democrats that our government is an organization that will be there for us even when our fellow citizens who see us as other seek to shut us out kick us out shut us down but in late August 2005 we those who live in the Gulf Coast we who have loved ones there we who have no connection to the area but watch on television learn that our government has had no plan for us.

Them Niggers should be grateful, she might as well have said. Here, have a hot dog. We gave you have a damn hot dog. Dog. Be grateful.

Pledge your allegiance.
Stand for it.
Stand.

XXXI.

I had no idea how much he meant to me until he was gone. Professor Kennell Jackson. My freshman year resident fellow who was so light-skinned he didn't even strike me as Black. He died of a degenerative pulmonary disease in November of 2005.

I'd never known quite what to make of Kennell that first year, or what he felt toward me for that matter. He'd glance at us freshmen, shake his head, articulate an observation we couldn't quite understand. He was quirky. Eccentric. Opinionated. Obviously brilliant. There were over 160 of us in his dorm, and that first quarter as I struggled academically, I just hoped to fly below his discerning radar.

By the end of sophomore year, I'd decided I wanted to be a resident assistant. Someone who'd help the new freshmen along. I wanted to serve on the Branner staff, always among the most popular staffing spots. I was selected along with ten others, and being on staff meant weekly meetings with Kennell.

The staff met with him every Monday night, sometimes late into the night if there was a particularly gnarly student situation to try to solve. Once or twice a quarter he'd enlist our help in making homemade chocolate chip cookies for the entire dorm, the scent wafting up to the second and third floors, into the grand lounge in the middle of the first floor, and over to the other side. He knew this was how to get the freshmen to meet one another, to pull them out of their new comfort zones of room and hall. He deployed a dozen stainless steel cookie sheets for the enormous undertaking.

He also wanted the dorm to be an intellectually rich environment and expected we, his staff, would convey that with our behavior and language. So he got annoyed at us when we goofed around, even when it was behind the scenes in his apartment, even when it was during cookie making—except for the times when *he* wanted to let his hair down and participate in the fun himself, or even start it. I never knew how to predict which Kennell we would get in any given moment. He was chummy with a few of the others on the staff though, joking around, inviting them on an errand to get delicious oranges at his favorite produce market, Sigona's.

I always seemed to be out of step around Kennell. His gruff, judging demeanor delivered his opinion on every big and little thing. Whenever

I opened my mouth around him I was afraid of being critiqued, so I opened my mouth as little as possible. Still, secretly I wanted him to like me, to show me with his liking that I was Black enough to be worthy of mattering.

Because I was majoring in American Studies I took a steady diet of American History classes. To know Kennell better, I branched out and took his Introduction to African History class, where I did very well on the papers and made comments in class he appreciated. One day in the lunch line at Branner, Kennell was a person or two ahead of me. I tried to dodge his gaze as I didn't feel like being particularly erudite at that moment, but he was tall and spotted me standing there. I heard him speak to the person between him and me. "I don't think Julie knows how smart she is."

Offended—I took the comment as criticism—I blurted out, "What are you talking about? Yes I do." He smiled, shook his head, and looked away, and I looked away too, not really sure what had happened, trying to replay his words in my head to discern a clearer meaning, but I couldn't.

Later, the *Stanford Review* would excoriate him for teaching a class on Black Hair, a course that not only acknowledged and explored an issue that mattered well beyond my personal struggles but that also, as it turned out, produced noteworthy research, by students, on the role of black barbers in America's Reconstruction and on other historical aspects of black hair and hair care.

Seventeen or eighteen years after that awkward conversation in the lunch line, I was dean of freshmen. The best resident fellow to ever hold the job at Stanford lay dying at the Stanford Hospital. And if I wasn't in his close circle of friends before, I certainly wasn't in that circle now. Then I heard from a colleague who had been to visit Kennell that day. "Kennell asked where you were."

Really?

I had to do this right.

He'd never asked me to go to Sigona's with him, and I had never in fact been to Sigona's in my life, but now I went of my own volition to Sigona's and selected the two most plump oranges I could find. Then I drove over to the hospital a few streets away. I found the door to his room and looked around but saw no one else I recognized, no one who could provide ballast in case Kennell was in one of his moods. I took a deep breath and rapped my knuckles on the door.

He barked his voice at the intrusion. "Who is it?!" I shuddered and whispered loudly, "It's Julie." I pushed the door slightly open. "Good, good, come in," he said. "I was wondering when you were going to come." A colleague from the English Department was sitting quietly in a chair against the side wall. I began to try to explain why I hadn't come before but didn't know how to finish the sentence. *How do you say to someone I didn't think you'd want to see me as you lay dying?*

I went over to Kennell's bedside and kissed him on the cheek, a far more intimate gesture than we'd ever exchanged before. I held up an orange and said I'd just been to Sigona's and did he want some? "Yeah, yeah." He smiled, and then he began to cough. I peeled the orange as a nurse came and tended him.

I sat at his bedside and fed him bits of orange sections until he'd had enough, and then I pulled the bedside chair over to the foot of his bed. It was easier to make eye contact from that angle. His long lanky legs filled the entire bed and I asked him if he wanted me to rub his feet. He did. I'd been here before, it seemed, with Stephen and Daddy a decade earlier. And I'd learned from watching those two men die that dying people don't want to be treated like they're dying. And on top of that, this was Kennell. I knew that if my presence was to be useful, I had to bring my A game, talk about what was going on in the world, act nonplussed by the tubes and chirping machines.

The next day when I visited he was asleep. I watched the tubes inflate his withering lungs from my spot at the foot of his bed. I sat with him for a while.

The day following he was awake and alert, and with some urgency he told me he wanted me to organize his memorial service. He had specific ideas for the music, the program, the people I was to invite to speak or perform. I took it all down like he was my boss telling me to plan a project, a task that made me feel for the first time adequate in his eyes, like he'd been putting me through a trial all these years and I'd come out the other side. Like maybe the trial had been mostly in my mind. He'd never been tolerant of emotion. When he said he wanted me to speak on behalf of the RAs, I closed my eyes and scrunched up my mouth so as not to cry.

He died about a week later. We held the service the following January to coincide with the Martin Luther King Day holiday. As I sat in the second pew behind family, pressed shoulder to shoulder with my fellow Branner RAs, listening to others' stories about how he'd impacted their lives, my tears steadily fell. Kennell had been trying to tell me, not just in an awkward conversation in the dining hall years ago but in the years before that and since, *Stop stumbling over yourself. Get out there. Go and get it. I see you, girl. You got this. You belong.*

XXXII.

After Kennell died, Dan and I filled in as Resident Fellows for the remainder of the 2005–6 school year while the university searched for a permanent replacement for him. We joined the effort to pack up his belongings. The colleague in charge of this effort invited me to take anything that was meaningful to me. I went searching for the cookie pans.

They were in the cabinet under the kitchen sink, a stack of twelve of which I took four. Also under the sink, in the far back corner, there was a large object wrapped in newspaper. I crouched down, reached in and grabbed it, and stood up again holding it in my hands.

The mysterious package was wrapped in eight or ten sheets of newspaper, water-stained in one small spot but otherwise as crisp as the day it was published. What could it be, I wondered, this treasure wrapped with some care yet forgotten under the kitchen sink? To look further felt like prying. But the only person who would care about that was gone.

I pulled back the paper and let it fall to the floor and stood holding an unremarkable object: a medium-sized metal colander with two metal handles, painted reddish-orange flecked with tiny dots of white. I began to imagine that Kennell must have retired it from use when he updated his kitchen décor. Or maybe it was a gift he'd never liked, never used. He had always been particular that way. I decided to keep it and set it on the counter on top of the cookie pans. Then I bent and gathered the newspaper.

The masthead caught my eye. Then the headline. Then the date. A sound forced its way up and out of me, like the gulp of a drowning person or the gasp from sudden injury, such that Dan in the next room overheard and came around the corner to see if I was all right. He found me sitting on the floor, clutching the September 23, 1985, issue of the *Stanford Daily*—the issue that welcomed my freshman class to campus. I leaned my head back against the cabinet and felt God or Kennell or some existential purpose for all of this comforting me like a blanket.

XXXIII.

A few weeks later something happened that made me realize I might be ashamed to have such a light-skinned daughter. I was thirty-eight.

I was headed to a late afternoon holiday event hosted by a group of mostly Black colleagues, colleagues I had begun to befriend, and with whom I was hoping to make up for the lost years earlier in my life when there were no Black people around. I wanted desperately to go to this party. Not just to go, but to walk in and maybe see a few faces turn and smile and wave me over. They'd invite me to sit. We'd talk. We'd laugh. I'd be accepted as one of them. This was as real a possibility to me as any dream.

But I am on kid-duty that afternoon, which means I will have to bring Sawyer and Avery, now aged six and four, with me to the event. I want to attend so badly, yet I know, in bringing my girl with her light olive skin and shiny, smooth, wavy brown hair, that she will be the tangible evidence that I had not only chosen to marry a white man but that I hadn't been Black enough to pass along Blacker genes to both of my offspring.

By the time I drive up to the event in my minivan and get one kid then the other out of their car seats, a feeling of dread is starting to crawl up my leg bones and into my stomach. Holding a child's hand in each of mine, I fumble with the key fob that automatically shuts the minivan's wide door, and then I begin walking with my little ones through the parking lot toward a meeting room in Tresidder Memorial Union.

We enter the big building and walk the linoleum floor, a familiar walk—I attend meetings here many days a week—but I feel out of place as if I am making this trek for the first time.

We get to the room and through its glass doors I can see my colleagues, smiling. Chitchatting. Someone is playing the piano. Trays of hot food sit on round tables covered in gold cloth. I pushed the glass door open and in a soft voice urge my boy and then my girl to walk through. I bring up the rear behind them, the tiny hairs on the back of my neck stiff as I nudge their small bodies in the direction of the most familiar face in the room.

XXXIV.

Viewing that holiday party scene from a distance of more than ten years, I shudder at having taken my children so close to the deepest cavern of my psyche. Were they blissfully unaware of the anxiety roiling within me? Or could they sense it, the unease flooding me as we walked through the glass doors of that holiday party? Fear comes not only with behavior—fight or flight—but with a scent, strong and acrid. Could my children smell it pouring off me, coating not only their little heads and bodies but the air all around them?

Professionally, I appeared to have taken all the right steps. I had degrees from elite schools. I'd landed prestigious work. I'd done all of this schooling, all of this work, in part so as never to be called Nigger again. But I walked tentatively through my life, unstable, feeling a hollowness inside, as if the very construct of my self was liable to fracture into pieces and fall apart. At any moment I felt I might step on a crack, break my own back.

In the Oak Lounge at Tresidder Memorial Student Union I worried intently about how my Black colleagues might treat my younger child with her pale visage; even a third-rate psychologist would have said the only real harm to my child was lurking within me. And in actuality my colleagues greeted me kindly, cooed over my kids, and no one looked sideways at my girl.

The day after the holiday party I sat down with my laptop, where, propelled by a deep fear of the person I may have become, fueled by an aversion toward the mother it looked like I might be, for the first time in my life I banged out a piece of prose that wasn't for school or work.

"She looks so unlike me, so unlike what I expected . . ."

Through writing I tried to stare straight into my heart, to examine it, to get closer, and even to hold my heart in my hands. When I did so, what I found was flesh partially covered with a scab still trying to form over a long-festering wound. I took a deep breath, then I poked the scab and picked at it, then pressed hard and watched what happened. The pus oozed out thick as toothpaste. And when it was done oozing, it had formed a word: Nigger.

I wrote that shit down.

I knew the infection of self-loathing was bad and deep, likely to spread to my precious girl child if I didn't find a way to get it out of me. I gave myself permission to tell myself that the birthday locker incident had in fact happened. I dared to tell the truth of it inside my head, dared to put it on the page, dared to write it down. Dared to stare at the word some anonymous white American had called me. And to take a deep breath and see that I still lived.

And why the challenge with Avery? I felt her lightness lessened my Blackness among Blacks; I could never pass as white and now, because of her, I couldn't pass as Black either. This tiny child kicked me deep into a racial crevice, with no ledge to hold on to. I want to drag a Black cloak over my white-looking daughter. To build Black consciousness in a child the world would see as white, by un-hiding her Blackness, by trying to hide her whiteness. So that she'll love the skin her Black ancestors are in, so she will not sit silently, passing, when someone says "Nigger," so when she gets asked the "What are you?" question, she'll claim herself as belonging to me. I even want my girl to be called a Nigger. I want when she hears that for her to know Blackness includes her, too. I want her not to be embarrassed by the Blackness of me as I was once embarrassed by the Blackness of Daddy.

I need a girl child labeled like me so I can feel less alone.

I was extremely fucked up, maybe so fucked up that I might harm my child psychologically. I never wanted Avery to fear that she was anything other than exactly what I'd wanted in a daughter. It was on me to be the mother she deserved. It was on me to work out this race shit.

By the end of the exercise—an essay of some length I revised and revised and revised for months, I'd finally reached an essential truth.

I wasn't ashamed about Avery.
I was ashamed to be me.

EMERGING

I.

My first class of freshmen is graduating in June of 2006, and in April I receive an invitation from Jan Barker-Alexander, the Associate Dean of Students and Director of the Black Community Services Center, to attend the annual "Black Graduation" ceremony.

I hadn't attended my own "Black Grad" seventeen years earlier, then called Black Baccalaureate, for fear of being not Black enough and therefore not welcome. Afraid of showing up with my white mother in tow. How would that go over? But now it seems I am wanted, not only to support the students but to sit up on that large stage in a place of honor with the other Black senior administrators and Black faculty. I feel giddy, like I've been invited to prom by the cutest kid in my class. I feel the nerves that come from doing something important for the first time.

I tell myself to get over it. I am a dean. The graduation isn't about me or my impure ancestry or my fragile history with Blackness. It is about being there to celebrate other people's kids, many of whom I know quite well. I go, having no clue what the experience is about to do to me.

Although it would move to a bigger venue the year following, this year, Black Grad takes place in Memorial Church, a domed sandstone and stained glass structure that sits at the center of campus and feels like its heart. The event begins with drumming, and we, the faculty and staff, wait until all of the guests are seated, then we process down the long aisle two by two. With a couple hundred Black graduates—bachelors, masters, and doctoral candidates—plus families of various sizes, and faculty and staff in attendance, the place is packed to standing room only.

The graduates-to-be sit down in front during the speeches and drumming performance, and then the event everyone waits for—the Kente cloth ceremony—begins. The students rise from their seats and line up in alphabetical order against the far left wall. The parents or other family members do the same on the right. Then one by one by one, as Dean Jan Barker-Alexander reads out the names, the students and parents ascend the left and right steps, respectively, walk across the wide dais toward one another, and meet in the middle. There, the student kneels or bends or stands straight up, depending on their height, to receive the woven strip of Kente cloth. Carefully, the parent drapes the long, thin cloth around their child's neck, like a scarf. Faculty and senior administrators seated on the dais oversee the Kente cloth hooding ceremony like elders. The students and their family members cross directly in front of us.

We don't wear Kente—the traditional embroidered cloth of the Ashanti people of Ghana—because we're Ghanaian. After all, we rarely know whether we are or aren't. We were taken from whatever our home nation was, sold into slavery, brought through the Middle Passage to North America, the Caribbean, and South America. The history and ancestry and culture from whence we came were systematically erased from us, beaten out of our minds if not our bodies, evident only—perhaps, if we can afford to discover it—in our DNA.

Most of us likely are *not* Ghanaians. But that is not the point of our wearing Kente. Ghana's port city Cape Coast served as a main export site for slaves, a funnel if you will, delivering slaves from the continent into holding pens, onto boats, and over the Atlantic. For many of our African ancestors, regardless of which country they hailed from, Ghana was the last African ground they touched. Wearing Kente is like being in the arms of a long-lost grandmother who has found us and has called us home.

There I sit on the huge stage, facing the crowd of fifteen hundred, wearing the robe representing my highest degree with its black velvet hat and tassel, watching the sons and daughters of the African Diaspora process in front of me, to be greeted with the most wide smiles of love by their parents, to be gifted with the cloth of long-ago ancestry. That alone might have put me over the edge emotionally as I sat watching my first Black Grad, and I did chase tears from my eyes as Jan read not only the names of each graduate, but their degree, which became a call-and-response cadence with the audience's loud applause.

"Bachelor of Arts in History"
"PhD in Chemistry . . . Stanford's first!"
"Double Major in Economics and African American History"
"Phi. Beta. Kappa." Jan always punctuated that one slowly for maximum effect.

All of this achievement, this excellence, among Blackness is so beautiful to see. I wipe my eyes, repeatedly.

But what really gets me are the family members. A Nigerian couple in exquisite silk robes takes the stage and I'm catapulted back in time. Having been born in Nigeria, outside my immediate family Nigerians were the first people I ever knew. I tear up at the audience's wild applause for these people.

Then comes a single black woman, thin and frail, walking with the effort of age to greet who I presume is her grandchild. I keep pushing tears off my cheeks as the audience continues its thunderous applause. Then I look over to the staircase at the family waiting to go next. It's a white woman and a Black man. I gasp and hold my breath. *Oh Jesus, an interracial couple. What will the crowd think of them?*

This couple, looking uncannily like my own parents, cross the stage with huge smiles and greet their caramel-skinned boy child who is also grinning. They walk as this crowd continues its thunderous applause. And I'm sitting in my chair on the stage with tears streaming down my face, my nose clogged with snot. I can't even bring myself to clap as I'd been doing for everyone before. A faculty member three seats down passes me his cloth handkerchief, and I clutch it gratefully, desperate to continue to watch before wiping these tears. I manage a few claps as they walk together off the stage. The moment is over and it's the next graduate's turn.

What began to sprout in me that night was a sense that a biracial person could belong within Blackness. The applause for an interracial couple and their kid, willingly, lovingly offered by more than a thousand Blacks, was unambiguous recognition of the existence of interracial families and light brown kids. Not just recognition but approval.

They see me. I'm good enough as is. I don't have to fear I'm not Black enough. I belong.

It felt like the most religious of baptisms.

II.

The following fall at New Student Orientation I go to the Black Community welcome and sit up a bit straighter in my chair than I'd done in years past. Student leaders offer words of welcome to the new students and their families, then Jan gives her remarks to the crowd.

"Welcome to the Black community at Stanford. We are African, we are African American. We are Multi-racial, Biracial, Caribbean. We are from the East West North and South. We are gay, we are straight. We are Muslim, Christian, Jewish, atheist, agnostic. We are first generation educated and we are third generation. We eat sushi, and we eat collard greens too. I don't know what 'acting Black' is, but the one thing that Black means here at Stanford is excellence."

Although she'd been opening like this for years, this time I actually hear her words, and I inhale them deep into me. After Jan speaks, she asks all of us Black staff and faculty in the room to stand up front in a line and introduce ourselves. Now in my fifth year as dean of freshmen, I know a slew of the upperclassmen in the room. When my turn to speak comes, they will show me some love with their applause, I know. As I wait for the mic to be passed to me, I don't think about the "whiteness" of my voice or my shaggy biracial coils, which are now so long they touch my shoulders.

One of our new freshmen that year is from South Central L.A. A student who had graduated high school at the top of his class, who will play football for us, who will champ at the bit to prove to coach Jim Harbaugh just how good he is on the field, and who will go on to play cornerback for the Seahawks and become a beloved figure in Seattle. His name is Richard Sherman.

III.

Back at my office, I'm still in a bit of a tense dance with the colleagues with whom I've tried to press my points about what's right for our freshmen. In November 2006 the vice provost brings in an executive coach to work individually with each of us and to improve our team dynamics. The coach is a woman named Maryellen Myers, a white Buddhist aikido master. Frankly, I look forward to helping her discern what is wrong with each of my colleagues.

IV.

One day the four of us who report to the vice provost—all of us women, the other three white—are meeting in a conference room to strategize over how to present a sticky issue to him. Janine, who is seated next to me at the table, interrupts our conversation and abruptly turns her body ninety degrees to face me. Janine is a thin white woman in her fifties of Eastern European origin with a perpetual expression of mild annoyance and a reputation for being impatient. Junior people walk on eggshells around her. But she seems to like me. More than that, she seems to believe in the changes I am trying to bring about as dean of freshmen. She is tough and fair, and I admire that about her. I am used to being able to spar with such people and win or at least draw.

Now staring at me with a broad smile, Janine widens her eyes in delight, presses her palms down onto her thighs, and blurts out that my hair is "so interesting," even "amazing." Then she reaches out to touch it, at first patting it with both of her hands, then bouncing and lifting it like a beach ball.

I shake my hair to rid it of her hands. I push my seat back, stand up from the table, and back away from her. "This is a thing," I say in a loud voice, both hands up in protest, looking around the room, appealing with my eyes for help from the one woman I hoped knew better. "This is a thing white women do to Black women. Treat us like zoo animals. I'm not a zoo animal. You're not supposed to pet me." My words splatter the room *tat-a-tat-tat-tat* like ammunition from a machine gun. My tone is emotional yet I am trying to smile so as to make it clear that I am not the bad guy here. My colleagues stare at me, their mouths open.

That day, I become the Angry Black Woman.

V.

In February 2007 Barack Obama announces he is running for President of the United States. I'd watched him speak at the Democratic National Convention three years prior and had physically lifted myself out of my chair that night, jubilant, like when I'm watching my team crush it in a big game.

I am getting restless in my career at Stanford, wondering how much longer the joy of working with the students will outweigh the annoyance of trying to effect change in an environment where change comes slowly. The day after Obama announces, I write a long letter to the folks at his campaign headquarters in Chicago and attach my résumé. Something in that letter piques their interest and that March they fly me to Chicago for a conversation. There I meet Betsy Myers and Analisa Lafontant, two white women overseeing the enormous task of bringing this unknown candidate to the consciousness of a party obsessed with Hillary Clinton. I tell them I want to play a grassroots role in California. They tell me they aren't opening any California offices. I plead on behalf of the largest state in the nation for us to matter to this campaign, and then, shutting up and listening to them, I finally understand: there will *be* no California campaign until they make it past Iowa, New Hampshire, South Carolina, and Nevada. They offer me a job with Chicago headquarters but I can't imagine uprooting my family or commuting two thousand miles to support such a long shot.

I resign myself to being a volunteer if and when the campaign ever makes it to California. This means staying where I am at least for a while, participating in the coaching, listening to what Maryellen has to say.

VI.

I didn't have a Black mother to teach me how to be in the world. But I found a literary Black mother in the poet Lucille Clifton.

By summer 2007 our Three Books freshman orientation program was in year four, and after the difficult conversations over *Possession* by Byatt, we'd long since given up trying to select books by committee. For the past few years it had been my job to select a faculty member who would choose the three authors and their books and moderate the event. For the 2007 program, the faculty moderator selected *Good Woman* by Lucille Clifton to be one of the three texts.

I'd hated poetry for its confounding barriers. Had barely ingested what little of it they fed me back in the English classes at Middleton High School. Couldn't make my way through the obscurity of poetic language, be it Whitman or Dickinson. Could barely make sense of Shakespeare last time I'd tried. Poetry was a locked gate I wasn't interested in trying to open.

But as dean I had to read all three books. I would be meeting the authors for lunch in advance of the program, and I'd have the honor of making opening remarks onstage. I began reading *Good Woman* out of obligation. An hour later I looked up at the clock. I'd been hooked.

> and if the man come to stop me
> in my own house
> naked in my own window
> saying I have offended him
> I have offended his
>
> Gods
>
> let him watch my black body
> push against my own glass

If she is possible. If these thoughts are possible, this language. Then maybe I am possible?

"Pourquoi es-tu noire?"
Because I am.

VII.

After about nine months of working with the vice provost and his direct reports, Maryellen has conducted a 360 review on each of us, and she is ready to tell me how I am regarded by my colleagues. By now I trust her enough to be able to listen to the feedback:

Too emotional. Too aggressive.

Might as well give me a list of stereotypes of women and Black people and Black women and tell me not to do any of those things.

She lets me continue.

Yes I have a tendency to blurt things out when I get really moved by something or frustrated but my emotion is warranted.

"Is it getting you what you want?"

When I practiced law, my passion and anger could be channeled into useful argument. But in academia? It seemed to just push people away. And then I'm the one who has to apologize.

"I want to know why I'm this way," I plead. "That could take twenty years of therapy," Maryellen says, chuckling. "How about we focus on *when* you're this way, so you can start to notice the emotion coming and then decide what, if anything, you want to do about it."

What, if anything, I want to do about it. Maryellen isn't siding with stereotype. She is telling me that my power lies in being in charge of my voice.

With Maryellen's help, I begin taking notice of my behavior. When I feel a strong emotion coming, instead of acting on it, I try to pay attention to what I am feeling and where I feel it in my body, and what triggered the feeling, and I write it all down. When these feelings arise in meetings with my colleagues, I have a little code for how to respond: "DDE," which stands for *Don't dwell, excel.* For weeks my meeting notes are littered with this tiny notation.

Over a few months of this close attention to my self—of mindfulness, some would call it—I begin to be able to sense emotion coming. I can then pause, ask myself what is going on, and tell myself I am okay, while the conversation around me keeps going.

I begin to see that the trigger is a feeling of being overlooked, doubted, or dismissed. I begin to see that my fear that I will be judged as not good enough makes me desperate to prove, constantly, that they are wrong. I begin to see that I can't control anyone else's opinion or behavior. I begin to see that the only thing I can be in control of, if I work hard at it, is myself. With Maryellen's guidance I begin to see that I can love and accept myself regardless of what others may or may not be thinking of me. I can choose whether to speak or not, to be silent or not, to go off on someone or not, rather than let those impulses simply happen to me. As her coaching begins to impact me, I feel renewed. With the help of a white Buddhist aikido master I begin to emerge into a healthy Black self.

VIII.

A day comes when I summon the guts to tell Maryellen one of my most painful secrets: that as a child I hated being Black and was afraid of Black people. This gut-spilling fear-sharing loosens up knots of shame in my psyche. Loosens the muscles not just in my mind but in my soul. Speaking this awful truth out loud through tears kneads the pain out of me. The relief feels astonishingly good.

I wake up the next day no longer feeling the vise grip that asked me to prove I was good enough *despite* being Black. I look in the mirror and allow myself to see not what whites *might* see or what they might *want* to see or what they might want *not* to see; not conforming to what *they* admire. To see my actual self.

To see the color of my face and body—paper bag brown in fall and spring, high yellow in winter, milk chocolate in summer—and accept that some in America see me as the "other," and being fine with that.

To see my skin and hair and hear my "white" speech, and decide that it is not up to some committee on Blackness to anoint me as Black.

It took me forty years to stop twisting and turning this way and that in response to how I feared and hoped people of both races would see me.

I drive to work that day having shed the loathing of my Black self and, by extension, of all Black people from my eyes, which had prevented me from really seeing other Black people. I look into the eyes of one, then another, and then another Black person, and I feel my heart swell with feelings like compassion, admiration, love, even desire. As if discovering their existence, their magnificence for the first time. It might as well have been the first time.

Like climbing out of a deep depression, I hadn't known I was this afflicted until I wasn't.

IX.

A history read about in textbooks, literature, poetry, and newspapers, seen in movies and on television, heard in stories, heard in song, becomes mine. I begin.

To feel one with my ancestor, the slave. To know of slavery's systemic dismemberment of Black agency, debasement of Black men, rape of Black women, destruction of the Black family. Know of the wringing of energy and life out of my forebears, and of how they were then thrown out like trash to litter the ground.

To know of the efforts of resistance, rebellion, and escape. To know that those with light skin who passed into the white world left behind community, family, solidarity, and self in joining the white world. To understand that most could not pass and endured wearing the skin God gave them. To know that the promise of God and heaven was at times the only balm.

To know emancipation meant freed from ownership by another human then consigned to a life where skin color equals less than, equals bad, equals thug, equals criminal, equals presumed guilty, equals justifiably frightens whites. Equals death.

To know we've fought and died for America since its inception, on this soil and on foreign soil, have liberated others in the name of America's ideals only to return home and still be called Nigger.

To know of the brief sunlight of Reconstruction. Like Greenwood in Tulsa. To know of the Black leaders including my own ancestors who began to shape a new way forward for us. To know of the rise of the Ku Klux Klan, of Jim Crow, of the uniquely American practice of hanging adults and children from trees, of the economic, social, and psychological re-enslavement of Black people. Of the new enslavement that is mass incarceration.

To know why a rational, educated, hardworking Black man living in the twentieth century hated that false marker of independence, that tribute to a time when our people were chained like dogs and cattle—the Fourth of July.

To see the face of Emmett Till, the child murdered because he may have winked his eye at a white woman, found bloated like a dead frog in a Mississippi stream in 1955. To see Emmett's fourteen-year-old face and see my own. To see my son.

To hear South Carolina's Susan Smith claim in 1994 that a Black man carjacked her vehicle with her two small boys in their car seats in the backseat and see this set off a nationwide manhunt for Black men, and to learn that Susan Smith herself had strapped her boys into their car seats, put her car in neutral, and let it roll into a lake, where her two small boys slowly drowned. To see white people not comprehend the psychological toll this takes on all Black people. This *Brutal Imagination*, as Cornelius Eady calls it.

To see the face of James Byrd Jr., chained to the back of a pickup truck in Jasper, Texas, in 1998 and dragged along an asphalt road for three miles, still conscious until his head was severed from his body.

To find a home in Black America.

Though later, when Trayvon Martin is murdered, and he looks to me just like my son, to know an even deeper *we*. A searing pain. A surer Blackness.

X.

I feel rage toward whites. I feel love toward my own people. I try to channel these emotions into something that might help someone.

And so what about this white husband and these quadroon children?

XI.

White Americans, you are infatuated with the Statue of Liberty whose tablet contains words of welcome for all, who did in fact welcome you and your ancestors, and you are simultaneously infatuated with carving lines and borders between who does and does not belong here, with yourselves on one side of the line and the other half of America on the other. You think your whiteness makes you better than the rest of us. You make us your scapegoat. Your excuse for your violent rage.

["It's not all of us, stop saying it's all of us," you say, my white brethren.] [You want to be treated as an individual instead of a stereotype.]

And I will get out of bed anyway and go out into the streets of America to do my work, to find true love, to raise children who know how to work hard and be kind to others. To speak.

XII.

In late summer of 2007 the Obama campaign finally stakes a claim in California with the grand opening of an office in Oakland—the first office located outside a swing state. When Obama himself comes to the Bill Graham Civic Auditorium in San Francisco that September, the Chicago team invites me to be one of the small handful of people introducing the candidate to his Northern California base.

It is heady, exhilarating, to be tasked with bringing a crowd of thousands to a rolling cadenced frenzy. I get a smiling nod from the candidate as he strolls out. At the conclusion of the event, one of the white women from headquarters takes me aside in the back hallway and thanks me, and then mentions a new constituency group they are forming—Black Women for Obama—and asks if I might want to lead it.

Yes, I desperately want to work for the campaign. But this role? No can do. I lack a connection to the broader Black community and to the network of important Black institutions like the church, sororities, and HBCUs. On top of that, Obama himself is contending with whether folks feel *he* is Black enough to garner support of Black people. I will not succeed at advancing this crucial cause.

I explain this to the woman.
"Is this about not being Black enough?"
Yes, I tell her.
And I am not ashamed.

For the first time in my life the truth that I am not Black enough for a particular role is just a fact, not a taunt. For the first time in my life, from my position inside Blackness, I consciously reflect upon what the Black people would want and need—deserve—instead of identifying with the white perception of something. Black Women for Obama deserves a better leader than I can be; I can say this plainly to this white woman without feeling inadequate or apologetic, even though I can see from the look in her eyes that she does not understand me.

XIII.

In my fortieth year, I stop letting whites pet me. When they try, without being the Angry Black Woman, I say simply, "Please don't. You shouldn't do that." I can save the Angry Black Woman for far more serious moments. Like when whites fear our unarmed children and kill our unarmed children, and when the system of white justice calls the shooter's fear of our unarmed children's brown skin reasonable and justified.

DECLARING

I.

To survive as a Black person in America, I have to assert that when
micro-aggressions penetrate my skin like a parasite, I will not let them
burrow deeper into me where they can eat me from the inside out.

What is a micro-aggression?

1. Getting to paw through a Black female colleague's hair
2. Commenting to others about how fascinating you find it
3. Calling the Black woman "angry" or "oversensitive" for minding
4. Not remembering this happened—or
5. Telling us to get over it.

When you feel us like a piece of fabric, it summons a genetic reminder
of standing there naked at auction, of being sized up and sold off
according to the size of our birthing hips and ripeness of our breasts.

II.

When I am forty-one, I see Barack Obama hoisted onto the shoulders upon shoulders upon shoulders of millions of Black Americans seeking to construct a human column of Blackness so high it can reach the light and maybe diffuse a bit of that light onto us all.

In 2009 President Obama is addressing a joint session of Congress about health care, when white Congressman Joe Wilson, a Republican from South Carolina, interrupts with two shouts of "You lie!"—an act of incivility, a lack of decorum that undermines the very office of the President of the United States. Joe Wilson might as well have called our President "boy."

When in 2012 Clint Eastwood speaks at the Republican National Convention and uses the prop of an empty chair beside him, which he speaks to as if it is Obama, the chair symbolizes the chair underneath the Black man about to be hanged from a Southern tree.

III.

In 2009, the PTA at my kids' elementary school throws a murder mystery party as a fund-raiser. My husband and I volunteer to work at the event, mostly to do our part to help the school, but also to get to know the broader parent community a little better.

Ours is a middle- to upper-middle-class neighborhood in Palo Alto, the heart of Silicon Valley. Stanford University is one of the largest employers in the area, along with big tech companies such as Google, Facebook, Oracle, and Apple. Our neighbors are mostly American whites and first- and second-generation Asian and Indian immigrants, a few European immigrants or expats, and a handful of Blacks, Latinos, and Native Americans. The neighborhood's politics lean heavily liberal. I represented our area at the 2008 Democratic National Convention as an elected delegate for Obama.

The party begins. The theme of the murder mystery is athletes marooned by a plane crash on a South Pacific island. Dan and I carry trays of food and drink from the kitchen to the backyard pool area where tiki torches help create an island feel. Lights float on the surface of the pool. Someone puts on some music. The guests begin to arrive.

One woman comes around the side of the house in Blackface. At first I don't really see what I'm seeing because I'm still bustling about trying to set things up according to the host's plans, and because I would never in a million years expect to see someone show up in Blackface. But there she is, jaunty in her athlete's uniform, skin burnished head to toe in a dark brown shoe polish, playing her assigned role of a Jamaican. Someone puts on some music. A white man assigned to play the part of "Tyrel," a track athlete, wears a huge Afro wig and begins to dance at the center of a circle of the partygoers. Another white man shouts, "Show us your jive dancing." The Blackface woman dances too.

I freeze watching these upper-middle-class white people, neighbors, and even a few friends drinking, laughing, goading the white man doing the mocking dance. The night is loud with music, hot with summer, and wild with this unleashed whiteness. Dan is watching from the other side of the crowd and looks over at me, his eyes wide with disbelief. I scan the crowd and see a Native American professor and his wife looking at each other. There are fifty whites and only a handful of us and they are drinking and laughing and egging each other on, and if I stand up and say something I am not certain enough of them even know my name so as to respect my voice if I turn off the music and shout *WHAT THE FUCK ARE YOU PEOPLE DOING.* I am more certain that if I turn off the music and say something, they will laugh and continue on with their frat party dancing.

I reel backward, fade away from the taunting crowd, with stomach bile jumping up into my esophagus.

Am I safe here I am not safe here this is not happening here this is happening and I need to leave and I need to leave now this is not happening.

I grab Dan's hand and we walk briskly away from the crowded backyard, through the house, and out the front door. I push the bile back down with deep breaths, fight back tears, ask myself if I dare to ask myself this question aloud.

Is this how white people act when we're not around?

I talk to the Native American professor. I write a letter to the school principal. Someone tells the Blackface woman that her getup offended me. She writes me saying she meant no offense. I Google "blackface" and send her the link. My doorbell rings and I open the door and suck in my breath as she stands there and apologizes in person. As far as I know no one ever said anything to Mister Jive Dancing. I make a point of never again going to parties thrown by white people I do not know well.

IV.

In 2012 Stanford's Human Resources Department is making a video to help orient new employees, and I am invited to participate in it. They want to portray my perspective as a dean and woman of color about the Stanford community.

I sit up straight in my chair under the hot lights and answer the producer's questions. Fifteen minutes later it is done.

"You're *so* articulate," the producer says, shaking my hand.
"Thanks."
"No, I mean it. You're just, I don't know, *somehow* incredibly articulate."
"You can't—Are we really going there? You shouldn't say that."

I am forty-four and have been a dean for ten years.

I am old enough not to take this shit anymore. I am old enough to remove the microphone clipped to my lapel, shake her hand while shaking my head, leave this small television studio, and walk confidently back to my office. I am old enough not to get emotional about it.

Holding my shit together is a victory as America works me over.

V.

While Obama is president, cell phone cameras pull back another curtain on what happens when we're not around: horrific violence toward Black people, even children. Cell phones make the whole world a witness. They carry the sounds of Black people crying for help. And dying.

Trayvon Martin, aged seventeen, buys Skittles and an Arizona iced tea at a 7-Eleven and is walking back to a family friend's home in an upper-middle-class white gated community in Sanford, Florida, when a neighborhood watch volunteer deems this unarmed, Skittle-toting hoodie-wearing teenager suspicious and deems that suspicion reasonable grounds to follow Trayvon, stop him, fight with him, shoot him, and kill him.

Darius Simmons, aged thirteen, is retrieving his family's trashcan from the curb one afternoon after school in Milwaukee and an elderly white neighbor shoots him dead in broad daylight. Darius's mother witnesses the entire incident.

Jordan Davis, aged seventeen, is riding in the backseat of a car that stops at a gas station in Jacksonville, Florida, rap music blaring from the car radio. A software developer who was in Jacksonville for a wedding considers the rap music in the car too loud and says so. Then he fires shots at the car, kills Jordan, and returns to his hotel and orders a pizza.

Jonathan Ferrell, aged twenty-four, is injured in a bad car crash in Charlotte, North Carolina. He drags himself out of the vehicle and walks down the street seeking help. When he knocks on the door of the first house he comes to, the white woman who answers decides Jonathan is a menacing Black man. She calls 911. When the cops come he approaches them, thinking they are there to offer him aid. A cop shoots him dead, firing ten times.

Tamir Rice, twelve, is playing with a toy gun in the park near his home in Cleveland, Ohio. He is shot by police and denied CPR and he dies lying on the ground at their feet, his toy gun nearby.

Oscar Grant and Michael Brown and Eric Garner and Freddie Gray, and Philando Castile and Alton Sterling, and Terence Crutcher and Keith Scott

and

VI.

I have been ashamed of America. America should be ashamed. America leveraged a slaveholding disregard for Black and brown skin to power its first industries. America built itself on the back of Blackness as a way to elevate the status of those with lighter skin. America owes Black people a debt of contrition and recompense. A process of truth telling and reconciliation.

VII.

We the people cannot continue to abide the stories of police and civilians on witness stands telling us that in just seeing our Black bodies they were terrified.

You have to be terrified for a justifiable reason.

God gave us this Black and brown skin. The skin God gave us is not a reason for you to be justifiably terrified.

VIII.

We are terrified.

Of you.

IX.

We continue to try to forgive.
To live.

X.

We do our work.

Ohio State professor Michelle Alexander writes of the mass incarceration of Blacks as *The New Jim Crow*.

Stanford professor Jennifer Eberhardt receives a MacArthur Fellowship, known as the "genius" award, for her research on the learned fear of dark skin. The seeing of brown skin that makes white folks—makes *all* folks—more likely to pull a trigger. The learned, presumably unlearnable, psychological cancer metastasizing in us all.

Journalist Ta-Nehisi Coates writes *Between the World and Me*, a letter to his Black son about whiteness—an invention designed to ensure a hierarchy of color—and about how to survive despite it.

Poet Claudia Rankine puts Trayvon's hoodie on the cover of *Citizen*.

Dan and I have "The Talk" with Sawyer.

XI.

On September 19, 2013, I'm in the lineup to read at the Cat Club, a
bar in San Francisco. Jonathan Ferrell has just been murdered by police
after surviving a car crash.

here is going on a war there is war on going on here
called him nigger.
called him liar.
hung Clint Eastwood chairs from southern trees.

blue red black
white ninety-nine
one stars and
bars stars and
stripes

invidisible

we may mass the troops amissing Sunday mornings
ammunition stackpiled on a stock of bibles

but just listen to the smalling voice of fearful white people—

i'm telling you:
stand up they are not going to stand for this take this sitting down

XII.

In August 2014 Darren Wilson, a police officer, shoots and kills unarmed eighteen-year-old convenience-store shopper Michael Brown in Ferguson, Missouri.

In October 2014, eighteen- to twenty-two-year-olds at Keene State College in New Hampshire erupt in a massive drunken riot and turn the campus into "a kind of war zone," which includes throwing billiard balls and full bottles of alcohol at the police, pulling street signs out of the ground, setting fires, overturning a car, and reportedly threatening to kill police officers.

No one calls these students thugs. Eighty-seven percent of the students at Keene State College are white. They are "kids" having fun at Halloween. The college president says his students have failed to "pumpkin responsibly."

XIII.

Even dying and in death we deserve no human mercy.

Eric Garner told police "I can't breathe" when they had him in a choke hold for selling cigarettes illegally.

Tamir Rice lay gasping for breath, his toy gun on the ground nearby, and the policemen standing over him did not offer CPR to this twelve-year-old boy they knew by then was only a child with a toy gun.

Trayvon Martin and Michael Brown were left dead on the sidewalk for hours, their bodies unclaimed, the local police do not even lift these boys' bodies off the sidewalk, do not properly care for the corpse.

The mothers frantically call, text, plead *Have you seen my son please help me find my son.*

XIV.

Trayvon shot no one. Neither did Tamir, nor did Michael. But the white supremacist Dylann Roof, who went to a Bible study at a Black church so that he could shoot people and did shoot people in a church, shot his gun off in a church and killed nine people and then fled, and when he was apprehended, Dylann Roof, the white supremacist, the police got him a Burger King cheeseburger because he was hungry.

The Black family members of the nine Black people slain in cold blood by Dylann Roof said in front of television cameras that they forgive Dylann Roof and they are commended for being able to forgive the white shooter Dylann Roof who opened fire at a Bible study meeting at Mother Emanuel Church and killed nine.

We know forgiveness is all there is in an America where we are not equal. Where we watch as our children are killed because of the color of their skin, and Dylann Roof, a self-professed white supremacist who systematically mowed down nine inside a church, flees the scene and later is apprehended and given a cheeseburger from Burger King, because the poor boy is hungry.

XV.

We watch.

We get up the next morning.

We give birth to baby boys whom Hollywood finds adorable and who show up in commercials and television shows and are coveted by white audiences for their cuteness and ten or fifteen years later we've raised those boys to be men who transition before white eyes into thugs.

Some of us live in middle- and upper-middle-class white communities thinking them safer, thinking them to be the place of arrival, of transcendence. We see Trayvon gunned down in a gated white community because he looked suspicious because his skin color and hoodie made him look suspicious and we gulp down our fear we who think we have passed into a better status with our money and privilege and degrees we gasp knowing we are wrong, know there is no place for us no place that is ours in America.

We have "The Talk" with our sons. Teach our sons how to kowtow to police. How not to draw attention to themselves. How to raise their hands in the air. How not to defend themselves even when they are sure they have done nothing wrong. How not to reach into their pockets for anything, not even to turn off their music. *Please, baby, remember: do not reach into your pocket to turn off your music.*

We teach them this while trying to also teach them to love themselves and not to be ashamed of their beautiful black bodies. Of their selves.

XVI.

It was inevitable that I would marry a white man. When Dan and I got married in 1992 I made an irrevocable choice that suited me well then.

Decades later, as a middle-aged Black woman and mother, I would examine not only what I'd gained by having a white man on my arm but what I'd irretrievably lost.

I see in my daughter's light skin the possibility of "passing," which I'd studied as an academic concept, a historical relic, in college and law school. What will this racial ambiguity do to her? Who will she be? Where will she locate a self to love? Where will she find belonging?

I see in my son—who looks out at me with soulful dark brown eyes like Trayvon Martin looks at all of us out from under his hoodie—a boy who cannot know what he might have learned if I'd given him a Black father.

XVII.

Identity is in part a response to the version of yourself that gets mirrored back to you. In *The Souls of Black Folk*, W. E. B. DuBois asks, "How does it feel to be a problem?" As Blacks we have a double consciousness, always looking at ourselves through the eyes of others, always aware that we may be the Nigger in the eyes of the stranger, the coworker, the neighbor, the acquaintance. And in our own eyes as well.

XVIII.

My daughter, Avery, is a teenager now and is more than I dared to dream she might be: smart, beautiful, fiercely sure of herself and also respectful, a ballet dancer, lithe and strong. When she lets down the bun her dance teachers require, her mixed-race hair curls and curls and curls down her back, her skin a light, light brown like butter just starting to cook in the pan.

I want her to be able to answer the "what are you" questions with the kind of educated pride that eluded me as a kid. I want her to be able to bring abject defiance into a situation when necessary. But over the course of her fifteen years, I'm fairly sure no white person has ever felt the need to ask that question of her. Instead, they are surprised to learn that the brown-skinned big brother she adores is in fact her brother, or that I am her mother. Which means white folks see her as one of them.

Crushing me like a tin can under some white foot.

XIX.

Sometimes as I try to raise these children up to love themselves and love others even I still loathe myself in my coffee-brown skin and frizzy hair and flatter nose and at the grocery store which is where I go weekly to get what lies beyond the cocoon of my home and I am muttering something to myself as I walk through the pasta aisle when I spot a middle-aged white man and I make eye contact with him or try but he averts his eyes from me and I realize that while a white man talking to himself in this town is a tech genius in this white man's eyes I am likely homeless or crazy in my ripped Harvard Law School T-shirt I must have gotten from Goodwill and when I get to the checkout lane I try to perform the part of a white person so they don't ask me for ID just like they didn't ask the white person in front of me for ID and I think no one has loathed themselves like I loathe myself and I am ashamed to admit this even to myself or into the air I exhale or to the other brown-skinned people but when I dare to tell it to the brown people for the first time in my life at forty-five after the murder of Trayvon and the acquittal of Zimmerman they look at me and their eyes well with tears and their soul reaches out to touch mine with an invisible hand and for the first time I realize I am not alone when I loathe myself as a Black person. Have never been alone.

XX.

We stand up for ourselves when we can.

XXI.

In 2014 when my girl is thirteen, we are visiting close family friends—a white couple my mother's age whom I refer to as Aunt and Uncle—in their stately home on the East Coast. Aunt Peg and I are drinking a glass of red wine in her gorgeous kitchen. Avery comes to get a glass of water from the tap. Avery leaves the room. Aunt Peg turns to me. "Isn't it great she doesn't look Black?" Aunt Peg takes a sip of her wine.

I feel short of breath. She may as well have said *Too bad you and your son are cursed with a skin of blackness.* I feel like I am underwater and might not make it to the surface in time.

I love this woman, have giggled with this woman, confided in this woman, and held her confidence once when she poured her deepest concern into me. I am also a guest in her home.

I have no idea what she intends by this comment. Maybe she's just doing her best to express compassion for what Sawyer faces as a Black male, and relief that Avery might, by those standards, have an easier time. In awkward race situations like this I've gained a lot of mileage by assuming the best intentions, by helping the white person not feel uncomfortable, but *Am I here to help others not feel uncomfortable?* I thought to myself. *If I say nothing, then nothing gets said.*

"Well no, actually, I mean, she is part Black. It's an important part of her ancestry." Aunt Peg goes on to say how her ancestors were from Scotland and Norway but none of that matters anymore and it is actually better that way. I say, "Yes it would be great if our ancestry 'didn't matter' in that it wasn't a negative in the eyes of others, but it *is* a negative in the eyes of others, it impacts our experience. And ancestry is who we are, it's who we're from. It's how we got here."

And I continued thinking silently to myself, *It's what ties us to something bigger than ourselves, it is our anchor and our stars, and these Black anchors, these Black stars, they matter to me. My slave ancestor Silvey died for me. If she hadn't been raped by that white man I wouldn't be here. And neither would my daughter. We need to honor her. We need to never forget Silvey.*

In the Black community we fight an internal war over our skin tone. We scrutinize. We chide each other for being too dark or for not being dark enough. If we're on the light end we pass the paper bag test or we don't. If we don't, we might just as well pass into the white community as our ancestors did during slavery and Jim Crow, exiling ourselves from Black folks, and therefore belonging nowhere and to no one, not even to our own selves. We are, at times, simultaneously ashamed to be Black because of what American society decided Black is and determined to be proud of who we are even in the face of America's hatred of us. We need as many people on our side as possible. It doesn't help when the light-skinned among us hide or even pass to the other side.

We are not turning from Black.

As I think these thoughts Aunt Peg is talking about color blindness.

I've loved this woman and felt loved by this woman for forty years, but that day when she held her wineglass in one hand and casually poked at the biggest button I've got with the other, I had to walk away. If ever there was a time I wanted to punch someone in the face, this was it.

XXII.

On June 10, 2015, the Black Lives Matter movement is front and center in our nation's consciousness as the police killings of Michael Brown in Ferguson, Missouri, Eric Garner on Staten Island in New York, and Freddie Gray in Baltimore, Maryland, are shaking a nation's sense of itself.

My first book, warning against the harms of helicopter parenting, had come out the day before, and a conservative radio talk show host named Laura Ingraham wants to have me on her show. Ingraham is one of the nation's most widely listened-to radio talk show hosts, a mother of three, and is known for "moving books." My publicist is wild over the opportunity. Ingraham is also a rabid Neocon who calls Black people "thugs." I decline.

My publicist pushes back. "This is a massive hit for the book at a critical time in the campaign. The Ingraham people say she only wants to talk to you about parenting."

I'm raising a son who is a human being of worth and value, not a thug, I tell her. Ingraham and those who speak like this over American airwaves put my son's life at risk with their vitriol. I decline.

My editor calls. My book is unlikely to be a *New York Times* bestseller if I don't do the interview, she tells me. Tells me the team of folks at the publishing house sat around the table and talked about this and they all agree I should do it.

"Are any of the people around your table Black?" I demand. "Are any of them brown? If not, then how about queer? If not that, then how about a religious Jew? You're asking me to do the equivalent of a Jew talking to a Holocaust denier. Find me someone who can relate to that and who wants to try to convince me."

My editor calls again, relays a message from the publisher at the very top of the food chain, who thinks it best that I do the interview.

I decline.

XXIII.

White people.

We win some small victories but America behaves as America does, and we experience small slights and enormous tragedies committed by you.

My nephew is a forty-one-year-old Black man and he was at your house the other day because he and your husband are old friends and he was in town for a meeting so he stayed with us but came over to your place to hang out for a long, long while and he left his shoes behind. (How does a man leave a house without his shoes is the kind of question often left in the wake of my nephew—my nephew who from the airport as he waits for his flight home to New York texted me *Can U get my shoes from my friend's house and mail them to me?*)

So I drive over to your house, which is in my neighborhood, and it is evening and it is dark and I park my car at the curb and make my way along the stepping-stones of your manicured walk and I ring the doorbell and to the left of the large door is a picture window with drapes only partly drawn against the dark night and from a warm living room your little blonde girl peers out at me and then turns around and tells you something. Then you answer the door and say quite sternly, "How can I help you," and I just want to pick up some fucking shoes left by my nephew at the home of his close friend and his wife but instead I perform.

"Hi, I'm Michael Lythcott's aunt Julie, I'm here—"
"What?"
"Yes, sorry to bother you, but I'm here to pick up my nephew Michael's shoes—
"Your—?"
"Yes, my—Michael, he apparently left his shoes?" I gesture to the pile of shoes visible in the foyer behind you. "He texted you, told you I'd be coming by to pick up his shoes. Or he called you?"

You hear the name of your close friend, my nephew, now for the third time. Your foreboding facial façade gradually falls away into a relaxed smile. "Oh yes of course," you say, stepping back, sweeping your hand across the vestibule of your doorway as if to invite me in, relief visibly slaking off your once-rigid body, and you point at a pile of shoes, where my nephew's lie indistinguishable in the heap of the shoes belonging to your family. And you make some statements about how you love my nephew and I plaster a false smile on my face, which you know is false, and my nephew's shoes are a size twelve and when you hand them to me they leave behind their absence, an absence you will stare at after I leave and even when you take your toe to the corner of your husband's shoe and kick it so it fills the space left by my nephew's you will remember my nephew's shoes.

XXIV.

My son, I look at the faces of Trayvon, Freddie, little Tamir who was all of twelve, and I see you, my son, my precious son, my beautiful Black boy, so smart and bookish and inquisitive and philosophical. I see you grow taller, grow muscles, grow a man's face, and I weep for the future self who will leave this home and discover that in pockets of this great country you are loathed, feared, and worse. My son, you did not ask to be born—I chose *you*. I asked you to be mine. I gave you a skin of brown.

And you are exquisite beyond measure.

BLACK LIVES MATTER

———————————

I.

Trayvon was my Pearl Harbor. The line demarcating before and after.
The moment I knew Blackness is the core chord in my life. Because

despite   imperfect
~~whatever~~ my ~~strange~~ history
~~inadequacies~~ with
      ~~as a person~~, Blackness
        ~~a Black person~~,
        ~~a~~
      ~~mother~~, my
        ~~inadequa~~

Because I am raising a Black son.

He was murdered on February 26, 2012, not in Ferguson but in
Sanford, Florida, a neighborhood a lot like mine. I read of it a few days
later in a small newspaper, weeks before March 17, which was when
the *New York Times* would pick up the story. The Zimmerman verdict
of "not guilty on all counts" came on July 13, 2013 and plunged like a
cannonball into the murky self-loathing in my psyche and displaced
every bit of that self-loathing, and the water that rushed back in its
wake was a torrent of bitter tears and anger, and the calm stillness
that followed was pure love. For my people. And for Trayvon.

When I see his face, all I see is my son.

II.

When your very existence defies the rules of the system into which you were born, you don't grow up respecting the rules. You want to fashion new rules where you can be one of the players instead of sitting forever out of bounds. That's the way I see it.

I am on the side of humans mattering. I take an interest in the experience of the other.

Perhaps I would have cared about these things even if I had been born a straight white male. But those were not the genes God asked me to inhabit.

I cannot look at his face. Years dead, years of justice not done, I cannot look at his brown face in that gray hoodie his dark eyes mournful like he'd come back in time as if he knew what was to come.

III.

Yes, sometimes, I regret the choice of a white husband.

To have given my son a father who cannot teach him how to be a Black man in America.

IV.

The more things change, the more they stay the same.

Richard Sherman, a cornerback for the Seattle Seahawks football team, says "thug" is the new N-word.

In the 2014 NFC Championship game between the Seattle Seahawks and the San Francisco 49ers, the final seconds were given over to Richard Sherman, formerly of Stanford, who leapt his body into the air to tip the ball from its intended receiver, Michael Crabtree, thus winning the game for the Seahawks and ending the season for the 49ers. When Sherman went over to shake Crabtree's hands, Crabtree grabbed Sherman's face mask and shoved him away. Then, as the game went to zeroes, Sherman made a "choke" sign at the 49ers quarterback, Colin Kaepernick. Then Sherman made a boastful statement to the ESPN reporter. Then folks got up in arms on social media over how poorly Richard Sherman had behaved. Pundits quickly labeled Richard a thug. Regular people and the media talked about Richard's behavior for weeks.

I take to Facebook to defend Richard, my former student, a man whose character I feel I know. I praise his ascent from the most challenging of beginnings in South Central L.A., I defend the chip he has on his shoulder from having to constantly overcome stereotype, I support his frustration at being undersold in the draft by Jim Harbaugh. A white male professor beloved by many of my former students comments, "Julie, I can't believe you're playing the race card."

It's not a card, I say. Not a game. It's our fucking life.

The following fall the white students at Keene State College who threw full bottles at cops and threatened to kill them later were just kids having a bit of fun.

V.

Richard Sherman is right.

Twitter trolls use coded language so they can spew white supremacist hatred and fly beneath Twitter's language regulations radar. My Facebook feed fills with white men and women casually referring to Black and brown men as thugs. Black and brown men looting stores in Ferguson are thugs, say these white people in my newsfeed, my so-called friends. White kids looting stores and overturning cars in New Hampshire are hooligans and pranksters and "kids who will be kids." Grown-ass white American athletes trashing a bathroom at the Rio Olympics are "kids." But Black and brown equals bad, lower, and you will call them thugs and your newscasters will call them thugs and we will cower in the corner of your imagined reality.

Richard Sherman is Trayvon Martin in a Seahawks jersey. He's straight outta Compton with a 4.2 high school GPA and a football scholarship to Stanford and a successful Stanford student and a professional football player and maybe this is not recognizable to you? That he can be all these things? Black and all these things? And if you don't recognize the Black person at your door as your neighbor or an athlete or an entertainer or as your professor or your president, if you don't recognize this person, you call the cops and when they come to your door, the cops will shoot the unrecognized Black person ten times or was it twelve and it wasn't the car accident that killed Jonathan Ferrell, this Florida A&M University football player, but the gun shot ten times and the 911 phone caller white lady presuming Black equals thug. Jonathan Ferrell's family buried their promising son and that white lady will never go to jail for her criminal behavior. Like Zimmerman's you call her fear of the Black man reasonable. Justified.

I kiss my Black teenaged son good night, night after night, lie awake in bed trying to figure out how to prepare him for life in "post-racial America" night after night after night.

VI.

I drive back into the night from your house with my nephew's shoes
suddenly feeling like an impostor in my own neighborhood. Thinking
what if instead of me my son had come to claim his cousin's shoes.

VII.

Even the Black man who was our forty-fourth President could not prevent a twelve-year-old Black boy from being gunned down as he played with a toy gun in broad daylight at a local park, could not prevent that Black boy from being denied CPR in the minutes he lay dying on the ground wishing for his mother, could not indict the police officer who felt brown skin meant credible threat.

VIII.

As Ta-Nehisi Coates makes scorchingly plain in *Between the World and Me*, America herself decided that he and I and people like us are lesser, with our brown skin, curly hair, thicker lips, and flat noses. Our status as the lesser is essential to America's narrative about herself; without us in the role of antagonist, there is no protagonist role for the white citizen. And this was no accident. America created the concept of race to justify enslaved labor, to steal its name, to bend it to its will, to strip it of its dignity.

It them us.

Some whites cling to racist leaders and racism itself so as to assuage themselves that however shitty their life is, at least they are not Black.

IX.

Some think we Blacks have actually gotten *more* than our due, like we have it easier than them because of antidiscrimination laws in employment, housing, and education. They call our efforts at linguistic inclusion and kindness "political correctness." And they're not about to accept a linguistic phrase—Black Lives Matter—that suggests that we need even *more* rights. That's how they see it. When in fact:

1. For the group whose historical and unexamined privilege is slowly eroding, the increasing equality of others can feel like oppression.

2. Black kids get shot by police and white kids get warnings. To pretend otherwise is to willingly not see.

X.

In my family we're one degree of separation from white rednecks and Black Panthers. How am I supposed to have that race conversation "we all know we need to have" when I can't even talk to my relatives?

In the quaint days before social media, we could keep our differences largely to ourselves and avoid awkward disagreements with our blood and married kin. When we did find ourselves captive before crazy Uncle So-and-so at the occasional family event, we could either walk away and find someone to commiserate with or choose to stay and defend a different perspective. At least we had to look each other in the eye, and if not in the eye, then at least we had to deliberately look past each other as we walked away, our body language passively communicating a bit about our perspective.

It's all different now, in the age of social media, where on any given day an uncle posts that I should really give Trump a chance, and a sister-in-law harrumphs "all lives matter" as she reposts something written by "Southern and Blessed." I find myself thinking, *How the fuck am I related to this person?* They're probably thinking the same about me. I want to shake them, shake the lack of disregard for the Black reality out of them, force them to look my Black son in the eyes and say that to his face.

Instead, I respond that we say "Black lives matter" not to mean "*only* Black lives matter" but to mean "Black lives matter, *too*" in a time when a Black teenager carrying a bag of Skittles home from the local convenience store is regarded as suspicious and gunned down as he struggles to defend himself, then left dead on the sidewalk, unattended to even in death.

You don't have to worry about that with your son, I remind my sister-in-law, reminding her also of her nephew, *my* son, whose very right to walk down the street unafraid is in jeopardy as others fear him and those who look like him and take up their guns accordingly.

XI.

You think if given the choice any of us would have *asked* to be born
Black in America? You think we *want* to be the object of your evident
fear as you pass us on streets and crowd away from us on elevators? In
the wake of the Zimmerman verdict Questlove wrote so hauntingly
about this. He described himself as a six-foot-two, three-hundred-pound
Black man, and pleaded, "I mean, what can I do? I have to be somewhere
on Earth, correct?"

Correct.

XII.

Sometimes I do wonder where is God in all of this?

I almost vomited when I heard an American doctor thank God for saving him from Ebola. It was the fall of 2014—those terrible few months when the scourge of Ebola had once again reared its head in a few African countries, and we Americans were fearful that, despite our best efforts at isolation, an African plague could invade our borders. A Liberian man named Thomas Eric Duncan had already succumbed to it here in the U.S. while visiting family, after showing up with symptoms summarily disregarded in the Dallas hospital where he sought help. By the time anyone realized he was more than a Black guy with a fever, the disease had consumed him as it does any victim, eating him from the inside out. Liquefying him. The hospital has since apologized to Duncan's family for systemically denying him adequate health care.

But the same tragic fate was not met by this white American doctor—Dr. Kent Brantly—I heard on NPR one day. Brantly had become infected with Ebola while treating patients in Liberia and had been airlifted back home to become the first Ebola patient ever successfully treated in the United States. Emerging as the survivor, the victor, from his intense treatment at Emory Hospital in Atlanta, they held a news conference for him, where he stood behind a podium with his enormous team of doctors and nurses behind him and declared that "God saved my life." And what went unstated but implied was that God didn't give a shit about the 1,350 Africans who had already died of the disease in its recent epidemic to date.

To be an American is to see God's hand in the U.S. health care system, and in the experimental serum known as ZMapp, which Brantly was the first human ever to try. To be an American is to believe God plays favorites, and that of all his children, he favors Americans most of the time.

To be truly devout, though, is to be a family member of one of the nine Blacks murdered during Bible study at Mother Emanuel African Methodist Episcopal Church by self-professed white supremacist Dylann Roof, and to forgive Mr. Roof for killing their loved ones in a house of God where presumably God was watching.

XIII.

Maybe God did give us the choice. Maybe he gathered a group of souls and asked for volunteers. "Now who wants to go down there and inhabit a Black or brown body? Who wants to take that on? Who wants to live a life in America where you may be treated like the scum of the earth? Who will walk among white people and be their opportunity to learn compassion?" And the bravest souls looked around at each other and raised their hands.

XIV.

I'm a middle-aged woman, comfortably upper middle class, with two graduate degrees, a house, two cars, and a retirement account. But my diplomas and dollars are paper shields against the army with their guns and self-righteous vitriol about their status as the inheritors of America. I think it is not unreasonable to feel truly terrified.

Though I am Silvey's child.
One of the original Americans.
I belong here.
And I will not be terrified.

XV.

There is so much I wish I'd asked Daddy before he died. About the birds he and my mother loved to watch and feed I recall only *black-capped chickadee, tufted titmouse, robin, cardinal, goldfinch,* and *sparrow.* Of the flowers they cultivated in our front and backyard and visited every evening upon returning home from work, cocktails in hand, I recall only *Queen Anne's lace, chicory Cichorium, morning glory,* and *gardenia.* And the things I never even contemplated before he died, such as *What does it mean to belong in America? And What does it mean to be Black? And How do we live under the drainage pipe of white supremacy with its drip drip drip of poison into our hair, that oozes down into our eyes, into our nostrils, into our ears, into our mouths, our pores, our bones? How do we coexist with these white people fearing and hating us without fearing and hating ourselves? How do we laugh? How do we stop seeing their fear and their hatred as a mirror that shows us who we are? How do we look into a real mirror and love what we see?*

XVI.

In the summer of 2016 I read a white Baltimore police officer's confessional. But it's not what I am expecting.

He's married to a Black woman, and she is pregnant with their first child. During the months of her pregnancy, Freddie Gray is transported in the back of a Baltimore police van, handcuffed, but not tethered with a seat belt, and is unable to stop his body from flying around as the van bounces through the streets of Baltimore. Gray's spinal cord snapped during this ride. Gray died. No one was held responsible.

This Black woman wife of a white male Baltimore officer is pregnant, and neither she nor I nor God can predict the color of her unborn child's skin. Or its gender. And when a son is born to them, a son of the color of brown, which equals Blackness, this white male police officer is quoted in the *New York Times* as realizing he is now raising a Black son in Baltimore.

Then he confesses that until he had a Black son he saw the young Black kids hanging around on the street corners on his beat as juvenile-delinquents-in-the-making, and now he sees them just as kids. Just kids enjoying the last few days of summer. What one might call "normal."

And in the poignancy of this white man's realization that Blacks deserve to be seen just as normal humans I am reduced to angry, helpless tears. *Is this what it's going to take? All the racist white folks need to get some Blacks in their family? Is this why gay marriage took hold so quickly—prejudiced straights had a family member or a close friend who was gay? If whites produce brown progeny, can we once and for all breed the racism, the white supremacy, out of them?*

Dear God, can we?

XVII.

I sleep with a white man. But he's different from the officer I read about in the *New York Times*; my white man never once thought Black kids were thugs.

XVIII.

"Biracial," a term I once courted, turned out to be a fleeting lover. Racial intermixture may be a fine way to root out racism—over decades, perhaps centuries—but what of the biracial child who lives that existence? I've been that tragic mulatto.

I didn't tell my parents about the N-word written on my locker on my seventeenth birthday because I didn't want their pity. Didn't want them to feel badly that they'd given birth to me or plunked me down in an all-white town. Didn't want them to look differently at me. Didn't want to be a victim. But like many victims, I felt I'd brought it upon myself. Instead of telling anyone about it, I let it fester inside of me, let it chase me through college and law school and into the workplace beyond.

I spent most of my life trying not to be your Nigger.

XIX.

In the summer of 2016 a close white friend and I are sitting at a picnic table with a handful of others. She asks me to talk about what I'm writing about in *Real American*. She listens to a few of my stories then begins to cry and says how hard this is for her to hear. She puts her head down on the picnic table and begins sobbing. I shift from telling about Black pain to putting my hands softly on her shoulder to comfort her in her white pain thinking this is a thing and people write about it and I love her and know her intentions are so solid and she connects with humans so well, which just showed me even more that this is a thing. A real thing.

But time is short and I'd prefer to offer my compassion to the antagonists in the grand narrative of America who manage to get out there every day and hold their heads up. Daring to be a person. Daring to make a go of life. Daring to be an American.

Dear white people,

When you're sad about racism please have the decency not to cry for your selves.

XX.

It comes time to address things with my mother. She is seventy-seven: still strong but more tired now, still very self-reliant and so frustrated when needy. And still beautiful.

In my kitchen one day, I speak to her pointedly with the voice of a woman no longer afraid to confront her past, her accuser, her accused. "How could you choose to live in Verona? How *dare* you chide me for not having Black friends when you raised me in an all-white town?"

She looks at me and begins to cry. She doesn't try to say my experience wasn't what it was. She tries to reach out to me but I back away and throw my hands in the air.

"He said white boys will be your friends but will never date you," I thunder. "Then why the hell did we live there?" She starts to explain what Daddy was thinking. "It was his truth from the life he'd lived."

"I'm not interested in making this right for Daddy! This was *me. My* adolescence. If Daddy believed it was okay to plunk me down in an all-white town where 'no boy would date me,' he was *wrong*. What did that even mean? That I didn't deserve to date? That I didn't deserve to be loved?" I yell this at my mother who, with Daddy gone for more than twenty years, is the only parent I can make listen.

She says she knew it would be a problem for me to grow up without Black people around and wishes she could have stood up to Daddy on that choice. Tears stream down her face and through these tears she says she understands and that she is sorry.

"You *can't* understand."

She has never walked will never walk in these fucked-up mixed-race American shoes my mother says she does but she cannot understand.

But I believe that she wants to. All I can do is walk toward her and hug her and tell her I know she did the best she could to raise a Black daughter. Because she did.

Being a mother myself, I finally know this. I'll be given hell to pay myself one day from Sawyer or Avery or both.

XXI.

"The arc of the moral universe is long but it bends toward justice,"
Dr. Martin Luther King Jr. said.

America freed us from 250 years of slavery, set us free upon this land,
the only land we knew and yet the land was foreign and hostile, and
we were told to go, get on with it, live free. We were promised forty
acres and a mule, resources with which to start a life, resources that
never came. So we began with little more than our strong bodies to
carry us out into a foreign land without family structure, without
income, into twelve years of Reconstruction and with it we were allowed
to bond ourselves to our own families again, and have names that were
our own. We had hope in those years that we could find a bit of land
and shelter our families and give our children an education and find
love and live free of violence.

But we went about this work with our brown skin, and the band of
whites nursed on a milk of white supremacy was hardly ever at bay.
Fueled by a seething bitterness that we were daring to try to live as
their equals, they donned their hoods and their sheriff's badges and
spat on us, hanged us from trees, began the psychological enslavement
of terror and then enacted Jim Crow with its rules about where we
could and could not go. We were thought so repugnant that white
children were not to swim with us.

A childhood friend from my young years in Snedens Landing revealed
to me only recently that this once had happened to me. I was seven. It
was 1975. We were all swimming in the aboveground pool at her house
in Palisades. There was a knock at the door and Jim Wilson's dad was
standing on the porch. He'd got wind that a Black child was swimming
with his son. He came to claim his white child from the water I was
polluting with my presence.

Forty years later, on the day I am fending off the pressure to promote
my first book on the radio show of a neoconservative white woman, a
white male police officer is called to a pool party in McKinney, Texas,
where he grabs a bikini-clad Black teenage girl by the hair and throws
her to the ground and pins his knee into her back in broad summer
daylight. As she screams, he, called to the scene because Black kids
are swimming in a white neighborhood, takes this Black girl in a skimpy
bikini down like she is the calf in the rodeo and we can almost hear the
cowboys shouting, "Wahoo we got another one." "Blue lives" with black

guns clamp Black girls to the green grass, her body still wet with chlorine from her neighbor's pool.

We want to swim. Eat ice cream. Enjoy a barbecue. Go to school. Get a job. Find love. Laugh. Die in peace.

XXII.

You hiding there behind your draperies across the street, it was you acting like Zimmerman who called the cops about a "disturbance" in your neighborhood, you who said there were multiple juveniles who do not live in the area or "have permission to be there," which you know because you guard the white experience and you know who belongs at the pool and who does not.

It was you who saw a Black man getting into a nice car and decided he was stealing it and called the police who trailed him, pulled him over, and pounced five at a time on his twenty-five-year-old Black body, this former student of mine, this man now getting a PhD in Engineering at Northwestern driving his own damn car.

It is you who call your dogs who bring their dogs to bring us down. To keep America white. To buff us out of your existence.

You want to stand your ground.
Which means arm the whites.

XXIII.

In the fall of 2016 a white woman named Kate Riffle Roper posts on Facebook that as the mother of two Black children and three white children, she's seen up close and personal how differently the world treats Black children:

> Now my boys look like teenagers. Black teenagers. They are 13. Let me ask you these questions. Do store personnel follow your children when they are picking out their Gatorade flavors? They didn't follow my white kids. Do coffee shop employees interrogate your children about the credit card they are using to pay while you are in the bathroom? They didn't interrogate my white kids. When your kids trick-or-treat, dressed as a Ninja and a Clown, do they get asked who they are with and where they live, door after door? My white kids didn't get asked. Do your kids get pulled out of the TSA line time and again for additional screening? My white kids didn't. Do your kids get treated one way when they are standing alone but get treated a completely different way when you walk up? I mean a completely different way. My white kids didn't. Do shoe sales people ask if your kids' feet are clean before sizing them for shoes? No one asked me that with my white kids. Do complete strangers ask to touch your child's hair? Or ask about their penis size? Or ask if they are "from druggies"? No one did this with my white kids.

My God this was me, and this is now my child, I think, stifling a sob as I read the whole post of this white woman who chose to raise Black sons. Through the tears my heart swells with hope for Roper's two boys fortunate to grow up in such a woke white family.

Around the same time I'm reading this Glenn Beck has a heartfelt change of mind about Black people and says so and with his words tries to turn the larger tide of conservative whites. My heart surges with hope as well.

Then my hope ebbs, and the rage returns. These are not new appeals; we've been saying this for decades, for a century, for the entirety of our time on America's soil. They believe us only when white people vouch for us. Racism will never go away.

XXIV.

In mid-November 2016, I peek out from behind my curtains, each piece of news like a creaky stair bearing the weight of an intruder. It's coming.

"We won. Black lives DON'T matter."
"There's a new sheriff in town and we don't want your kind here."
"Make America white again."

A girl goes to school and sees the word "Nigger" scrawled on her locker.

XXV.

We need white allies.
I hate that we need white allies.
We need white allies.

XXVI.

In December 2016 the prosecution of a white North Charleston, South Carolina, police officer accused of shooting an unarmed Black man in the back ends in a mistrial. The officer shot Walter Scott in the back as Scott was running away and planted his Taser next to Scott's body, claiming Scott had stolen it from him. All this was caught on video. The evidence right there, naked to see if eyes are willing to see. But one juror could not see. One juror refused to see. Will not see that the officer's abject fear of a Black man was unjustifiable. Will unsee that the officer shot down Walter Scott as if he were a wild dog.

Dear America,
What would you have me tell my son?
Don't drive, son?
Don't go to Walgreens, son?
Don't be . . .
What.
Don't *be*?

ONWARD

I.

No, I was never white.

A conservative white male friend asks me on Facebook why I call myself Black when I am also white. "I know you love your white mother," he says, like it's evidence supporting his point. A white female writer friend wants me to talk about my whiteness in my memoir as well as my Blackness because I am biracial.

My whiteness?

The one-drop rule invented to preserve white supremacy and to perpetuate the population of slaves as more and more slaves were raped by masters and gave birth to lighter children says whiteness is pure and Blackness is a stain and therefore if you have even one drop of "Black blood" in your lineage, you are Black. Period. It is one of America's oldest rules and it holds to this day.

Yes, I adore my mother, and my white British aunts, uncles, and cousins with their cool accents, tiny cars, wry humor, and fondness for a pint or a cigarette. My relatives on my mother's side embraced my very dark, very tall, very American father back when it was truly an act of transgression to do so. And they show nothing but love to me, as well. But me, white? Never.

Because that store clerk doesn't see me as white. That doorman in the lobby of a high-rise apartment doesn't give me the white right of way. That neighbor in my own neighborhood thinks I am at her door to sell her something or do her harm instead of reclaim my nephew's shoes. I am not white because whites do not see will never see me as one of them.

And because I do not want to be.

II.

It is Christmas 1974. I'd just turned seven. My older siblings—now twenty-nine, twenty-eight, twenty-six, and twenty-four—are visiting us in Snedens Landing for the holidays. It is dinnertime and they are seated at our rectangular dining table wearing full-moon Afros and brightly colored wide-legged pants. They reconnect by jockeying to be the funniest, the most informed, the most profound. Then they tell inside jokes and start giggling about the nicknames they have for each other. I am the small child listening to the language of family, paying attention.

One of my brothers looks over at me. "What's your nickname, Julie?" I look up. "Bridge over troubled water."

They say we choose our time to be born. They say we choose our family. I am here to live this strange mixed-race Black experience in late twentieth- and early twenty-first-century America.

In the grand scheme of Blackness past and present, owing to light skin and a higher socioeconomic class, mine is a life of privilege that threatens to alienate me from the only people who would ever claim me as theirs. I work to bridge that distance and to never forget whom I'm from. I cannot change what I look like, but I have a choice about how to be.

This I know: Black or white, rich or poor, in the light of day and the dark of night we all cry out in anguish and in ecstasy. We all sweat, bleed, and dream. We all want our children to get home safely. And we all just want to know we matter.

To America.
To someone.

III.

I am drawn like a magnet to the little fuzzy-headed brown-skinned kids with white parents whom I see in restaurants, in airports, in malls. My body wants to go near, my soul wants to be a friend to a child who might be feeling lost on an island.

Instead I smile deeply at the children and at the parent. If the parent doesn't get why I'm smiling, I hope he or she will think, *Why is that woman smiling at me? What is she saying with that smile?*

I'm saying, *Please read up on this. Please have Black friends. Please don't make the mistakes my parents made. Please build some belonging to community. Please give this kid a chance to develop a healthy self.*

If the hair is done right I compliment the parent.

IV.

Yes my white friend cry your tears. I know your pain is real as you feel the weight of this history this present lodge in your stomach like a stone.

Go there. Feel it. Hold it. Seek to understand it. Come to me with an open heart and I will show you my own.

V.

In 2015 I take Mom back to Ghana, where she met Daddy, and we hire a driver who drives us to the very beach where Daddy proposed to her in 1965.

Four years after meeting at that party thrown by the Americans in Accra, Daddy took Mom for a drive in his Triumph down what was then called the road to Tema. The top was down. The sun was beginning its plummet into the Atlantic. Daddy pulled over at a little spot where a small rivulet emptied into the sea. He helped Mom out of the car and onto the sand, and they walked toward the ocean. They neared the water. The breeze that always came off the water at that time of day ruffled her hair. Daddy stopped, turned to Mom, spoke some words of love to her, and gave her his mother's ring.

The road to Tema is now called Labadi Beach Road, a two-lane highway littered with trash like a frontage road in any city. Our hired driver, Isaac, a local gentleman whose skin is dark like cobalt, and whose bald head gleams in the bright sun, becomes invested in helping two Americans find the very spot of this long-ago wedding proposal. After driving back and forth along the highway, Mom focuses on a small steel bridge and decides this is indeed the rivulet near where Daddy proposed. Isaac pulls off the road just past the bridge, and we get out of the car. The three of us walk for ten minutes along the hot sand toward the rivulet, toward the ocean.

"Yes, this is the spot. I'm sure of it," Mom tells me.
I can't speak.

I take out my phone and click the camera, framing the picture. The immense Atlantic Ocean roars its constant waves onto the shore behind her. Tears stream down her face. She smiles lopsidedly and points to her ring. I hand my phone to Isaac and jog a few paces toward Mom and I put my arm around her. Isaac takes a picture of this white woman and her light brown daughter, these American women visiting Ghana. And as I steady myself on the sand I have the unmistakable sensation that Daddy had once been here. I wonder if Daddy or Mom had contemplated my existence as they stood, giddy, in the bright sunlight on this vast expanse of unstable ground.

VI.

One day I'm talking with Avery, now fifteen, about the other names we might have given her.

"You shoulda named me Marin."
"That was on Dad's list. I didn't really like it."
"Well, I like it."
"Well, looking back I kinda think maybe I shoulda named you Silvey."
She pauses. And then, "I'll name my own daughter Silvey, Mom."

I know it's my job as her mom not to cry.

VII.

We have "The Talk" a few times with Sawyer as new incidents of violence against Black men and boys come to light. Sawyer's living grandparents, all white, express concern, and I am grateful.

But like any teenager, Sawyer feels immortal. I have a feeling that only his sense of immortality scaffolds him and prevents the weight of these Black deaths from crushing him.

It would be rational to keep him inside. To keep him from the clutch of the strangers who would endanger him. I choose not to keep him inside. I gave him life and I intend to let him live it.

VIII.

This white man I sleep with I love.

This white man who loved my Black hair before I did I love.

This white man to whom I gave Sawyer and Avery I love.

This white man without whom I would not have Sawyer and Avery I love.

I love how he worked part-time his entire career so as to be the primary parent of our children. How he looks with such pride upon Sawyer and Avery. How he develops his consciousness about the Black experience by reading, listening, watching, informing himself so he can be the best possible white father to our Black son. How he loves his daughter just as magnificently as my Daddy loved me.

How he loved me when I did not yet love myself.
And gazes at me with limitless love still.

IX.

In the summer of 1969 we moved from Lagos, Nigeria, to Manhattan. Daddy became a dean at Columbia University's medical school. Mom had just become a naturalized U.S. citizen. I was about eighteen months old.

We moved to a university building overlooking the Hudson River, into an apartment on the twenty-first floor. Lagos was a world away from this Manhattan high-rise in every sense. We'd had a single-family home in Lagos. We'd had next-door neighbors, a family with three little girls, named Dunni, Funmi, and Ronke. We'd had gardens in front, and out back there was a pool and a lawn where I roamed as I took my first steps in this world. Moonflower grew up and along the back fence.

Although I was too young to remember, Mom has told me this story so often over the years, it feels the memory is also mine:

We'd lived in Manhattan for about a week when one morning I wandered into the kitchen where Mom was doing dishes. I tugged on her skirt. "Friends, Mommy, friends," I said, looking up at her.

Mom had never lived in an apartment building before, or in America for that matter, and the when and how of friend-making in this new country, in this tall rectangle of boxed lives, was a bit of a bewilderment to her. But she took one look at me and could see that I was lonely. That of all the things I might be missing from our life in Lagos, what I was missing most was someone to play with.

She dressed me in a lovely little two-piece orange outfit of a tank top with a ruffled hem and pants that tapered at the ankle, and small sandals. She put on a dress made of cloth she'd bought at the bustling Jankara Market in Lagos. She packed a bag of things we'd need for our adventure—snacks, books, and toys. And down the elevator we went. There must be some children who live in this building, Mom thought, and the lobby is where we will find them.

The lobby was spacious and Mom plopped us down on a window seat facing the large bank of elevators forty feet away. I imagine we made quite a picture. She, a gorgeous woman of thirty years, with skin of copper brown stretched taut across her strong, slender frame, dressed in the Dutch wax print cloth worn throughout West Africa. Me, a dark brown toddler with big brown eyes and a fuzzy Afro of medium brown, with my legs in orange pants sticking straight out on the seat. Little shoes pointing to the sky.

We watched and waited. Each time an elevator door opened we looked up, hopeful. A half hour went by. And then, finally, it happened. An elevator opened and there stood a tall, young, white woman with a little girl about my age. Without saying anything to Mom, without even pausing to look at her, I scooched myself off the window seat, hit the ground, and ran toward this child with my arms outstretched, calling, "Friend! Friend!" I never once looked back.

Mom says she realized only in that moment that something terrible could happen. That this white American woman could put a protective arm around her child and gently steer her away from me. That I could be rejected, feel rejected, in the act of trying to make a friend. As I ran across the huge lobby toward this white stranger, with my arms outstretched, calling "Friend," it felt like an eternity to her, my mother recalls.

The little girl responded.

She opened her arms and ran toward me. We met mid-lobby and hugged each other, both of us now saying "Friend" over and over again. My mother, tears running down her cheeks, got up and walked toward the other woman.

Emily and her daughter Gabrielle became our fast friends. Emily introduced Mom to two other women, both of whom had children my age, and we formed a playgroup.

I want it to be this simple.

X.

Well before I knew how to love myself, and well before I had children, my Daddy was gone.

On some evenings when my house has grown quiet and dark while I've worked late into the night and when finally I'm tiptoeing up the stairs to my bedroom, I smell my dead father. I smell him as he was in the childhood of my memory, when the scent of his aerosol-sprayed Afro Sheen and the aroma of his many Marlboro cigarettes formed a musky cloak of oil and wood and safety.

As a child I would hear Daddy's deep bass voice call multiple times a day, "Baby, bring me my cigarettes." He'd glow as I neared him, and next he'd say, "Now give me some sugar." And I'd lean in to plant my tiny kiss on his large, weathered lips, hoping his breath would smell savory like fried eggs and bacon, or sweet from his scotch, and not like the stench of sleep on an unbrushed weekend morning.

When the cancer had inhabited much of his tall, lanky frame and he was finally ready to pass, my mother insisted that it was time to call us children home and permit the kind of emotional letdown he'd forbidden us to have in the five years since his diagnosis.

"But there'll be all that crying," he protested.
"Oh Daddy, they need that, don't you think? Don't you think it's time?"
"I'm not talking about them," he said.

It was prostate cancer, entirely avoidable as a death sentence for him, a doctor who understood the source of his discomfort, knew it was a symptom, an indication, but chose to ignore it, chose not to be a sick person, chose not to incur the pity of others, chose not to buy more time for himself or for us. Five years earlier, when I was just twenty-two, he'd told us of the diagnosis in a letter, and just as bluntly told us not to speak of it to anyone else including him.

My brothers and sister and I got called home on a Friday in early October 1995, late in the morning California time, and we drove or flew in from all over the U.S., my journey from San Francisco to Boston onto the puddle jumper plane to the small Island of Martha's Vineyard being one of the longest. By early Saturday morning we had all arrived on the Island and had made our way to their house in the middle of the woods. There were a dozen of us—we his children, our spouses and partners, our children, and my mother—and we gathered in the cool stillness of the room that had been Daddy's office but was now his dying place, kneeling shoulder to shoulder, lining the stiff hem of his hospital bed with a soft ribbon of family.

The floor we knelt on was covered in a thick, plush, wall-to-wall rug of dark turquoise, like the color of a Caribbean coast where the seafloor falls away to depths below. My parents' artifacts and art procured during years of living in Ghana and Nigeria filled this, his final bedroom. The chiwaras, a pair of antelopes carved into wood from Mali, hung behind his headboard. The carving of Sopona, the god who gave people smallpox, whom my father had courted, negotiated with, and brought to work along with himself and the other Western doctors, rather than in opposition to them, stood on a bookshelf. The big lady from Mali, rising three feet tall, carved of a dark wood and covered in black shoe polish as an additive, naked but for a string of grass-seed beads around her neck, stood by the doorway.

When I entered the room that Saturday morning, I saw Daddy in bed against the far wall looking more like ninety-three than his actual seventy-seven, shriveling before my eyes, almost entirely gray, this tall strong man who had once moved mountains, measles, smallpox, and bad people away; half the size I remembered. I gave him one last kiss, feeling the dryness of his lips, sensing the acrid smell of teeth, mouth, and tongue no longer brushed. "I'm here, Daddy. It's Julie," I bleated, like a small lamb. He couldn't talk or even smile, but his strong right arm lifted his hand a few inches off the bed, and for a long last moment I grasped those strong fingers that had once held my wobbly seat as I learned how to ride a bicycle.

Then I took my place kneeling on that plush rug with the others, attending his final minutes, my hands over his right arm outstretched atop the soft white sheet, the dark skin, the strong fingers. I'd seen him string a bird for the rotisserie with those fingers, seen him accidentally stab his other palm with a screwdriver that slipped off the screw. But now what I saw was the papery skin of a body already too big for the soul that was detaching itself, soon to fade away.

As his breathing turned raspy and jagged, I heard the more audible gasps and fervent prayers of the family, also kneeling, also touching his hands, caressing his feet beneath the sheet, rubbing the strong thighs that once propelled him forward in sprints with Jesse Owens. And then something—a force powerful like a magnet, insistent like a bite on a fishing line—tugged my head upward. And I saw in the air in front of me the dissipating smoke ring from one last Marlboro, or the small, discarded heather-gray feather of an invisible tufted titmouse or black-capped chickadee. And when I looked down again at Daddy he was gone from his body, disappeared into the air, into the room, into the past. His skin and bones lay like a suit of clothing on display at a rummage sale. I didn't need anyone to tell me he was dead.

The hospice nurse who had been keeping quiet in a corner stood and walked toward us, nodding her gentle, knowing gaze, telling us without language that he'd passed on. Then the weeping began, the mournful, awful wailing of survivors who could finally release what we'd been admonished to keep inside us for five years. The cries became a swell, a final song, a symphony of love for our father, grandfather, father-in-law, husband, and a song of anguish for ourselves.

But I wasn't crying. I was perplexed by what I'd seen, caught in numb wonder at that puff of smoke, that feather, that gray wisp of something I'd watched float into the air as he died.

I've only ever dabbled in religious tradition, and never really by choice. As a small child, I was made Presbyterian by my parents. They wanted me to be baptized as some form of Christian, and the Presbyterian church up at the top of Washington Spring Road in Snedens Landing would do fine. And I made myself Mormon as a young adult, really just to prove I could. And so as I sat with my dying father, I'd had no particular religious belief to set a context for me. But when my head was tugged upward and I saw the tuft of something, I knew really, without regard to any religious tradition, that I'd seen my father's soul, or his spirit, or the essence that had animated him these seventy-seven years, leave his body. Seeing this was like discovering that a magician really can perform magic instead of tricking the audience with a sleight of hand. I felt a kind of pure, openhearted, reassuring joy from the knowledge that he was no longer suffering, and I felt wonder at the thought that one day I, too, might pass like this. As others knelt in anguish, I experienced awe over a death that was, in the context of death, still death, yet exquisitely beautiful.

Then the smell came, as the body, no longer clenching muscles, no longer beholden to custom, propriety, or manners, made the final movement of its bowels and released the final flow of urine through the urethra. I quickly regained my senses and was embarrassed for him, my Daddy, this man of tremendous dignity and stature, this former Assistant Surgeon General of the United States, now reduced to skin and bones and shit and piss. We were encouraged to leave the room so the nurse could clean the body and prepare it for its travel to a morgue and then on to a crematorium. We filed out one by one, and as I walked, eyes downcast, I passed the three-foot-tall big lady from Mali who was standing near the door. I touched her shoulder as you touch the knob of a banister to steady yourself, or as you rub the knee of a famous bended copper statue in a museum or stately entryway as a way of permanently recording that you were there.

XI.

The big lady from Mali lives with me now. She stands on a carpeted landing at the halfway point between the first and second stories of my house, where the long run of the staircase turns left before it quickly bends left again and leads to the upstairs bedrooms. On some nights as I creep past her, I smell the musk of Afro Sheen and Marlboros as the oil in her wood exhales a deep sigh into the California night. Or maybe it's Daddy sitting right there beside her, watching me make my way in this life decades past the last time he spoke my name. Maybe it's Daddy, watching with what I hope is pride, the grandchildren with their coltish brown and light brown limbs bolt up the stairs, grandchildren who never had a chance to sit in the lap of this magnificent man. Maybe it's Daddy, watching with what I hope is still unconditional love, the daughter he thought could be Miss America.

ACKNOWLEDGMENTS

This book has a complicated provenance.

I began to write about race the day after the holiday party in 2005. I am grateful to the universe for bringing me to that awful intersection and pulling me through it.

I began writing poetry after reading Lucille Clifton's *Good Woman* in 2007. I am grateful to Ms. Clifton for lighting the way.

In 2012 I began an MFA at California College of the Arts where I spent a good deal of time writing about race. I wrote a poem on race in seven voices called "A Day at the Races" for Joseph Lease's class, and am grateful to Joseph for urging me to publish it.

In 2013 I published that poem in a journal cofounded by one of my former students, Tanaya Winder, called *As Us*, which features the work of indigenous and underrepresented women. I am grateful to Tanaya for giving me my start as a published poet, and for seeing in my nationless mixed-race experience some solidarity with the experience of displaced indigenous people.

In 2013 I adapted that poem into a script for San Francisco's Poets Theater run by Small Press Traffic. I am grateful to Small Press Traffic for the opportunity, to director Brandon Jackson for his vision and tenderness as he staged my words, to Kelsei Wharton for documenting the experience, and to each actor for their careful consciousness: Yvorn "Doc" Aswad, Alonzo Cook, Ashley Hill, Ruth Marks, Estelle Piper, Luke Taylor, and Saroya Whatley.

I continued writing about race at CCA with the urging and support of many classmates and faculty including Stephen Jamal Leeper, Donna de la Perrière, Judith Serin, Dodie Bellamy, and Faith Adiele.

This book emerged from my master's thesis at CCA, which I wrote under the guidance and direction of Juvenal Acosta and Faith Adiele. I am forever grateful to the two of you for all but forcing me to go there.

I am grateful to my brother Stephen Xavier Lythcott for writing about our slave ancestor, Silvey, and to Silvey herself and everyone in between her and me for being and enduring and ultimately giving me life. To my extended family. To my mother and father. To Avery, Sawyer, and my beloved, Dan.

And as ever, I am grateful to the people who turned this manuscript into a book: my editor and my agent, the fierce and fearless Barbara Jones and Kimberly Witherspoon, and their entire teams at Henry Holt and InkWell Management.

Listening and Learning

1. This book is packed with firsthand experiences, ranging from triumph to tragedy, all told from a Black and biracial woman's point of view. Were there moments that surprised you? What did you learn or newly encounter from seeing life through this woman's perspective?

2. There are many points in the book where Lythcott-Haims holds the trauma of an experience inside, rather than telling someone or having access to people in her life who would have believed and supported her. How would having allies nearby have affected the author's ability to see her painful experiences as true and as worthy of being heard?

3. Lythcott-Haims's life experiences are set against a backdrop of whiteness as the norm in the United States, and the assumption that it's preferable to brownness or Blackness. What do you see as the impact of this unspoken preference for whiteness on the author? How does this preference shape the popular contemporary American narrative?

4. Toward the end of the book, Lythcott-Haims writes, "No, I was never white." What does she mean? What does "being white" mean? Why could she have never been white?

5. Lythcott-Haims describes her memoir as a journey from self-loathing to self-love. When do you think her self-loathing took root, and when and how did she finally come to a true place of self-love?

Believing

6. Once, a reader told Lythcott-Haims, "I'm sad that you are so angry." What might this comment reveal about the speaker? Did you find anger in the book, and if so, what did that anger convey to you? In what ways might Lythcott-Haims's anger be justified? How can this type of anger be useful?

7. Tiny acts or interactions that make a person feel lesser—micro-aggressions—are explained and highlighted

Discussion Questions

throughout the book. What are some of the micro-aggressions Lythcott-Haims describes and why do they matter? How do you think a person who is on the receiving end of micro-aggressions should respond to them? What are some things people can do to avoid making micro-aggressive statements?

8. Lythcott-Haims has said she hopes that the book evokes empathy for Blackness, the Black body, Black mothers, Black children, and Black people generally. Did she succeed? If so, where did this book evoke empathy in you? Were these new feelings for you and if so, why? How did this text help you improve your racial awareness and empathy?

9. What parts were harder to imagine or empathize with? Why do you think that is?

10. Lythcott-Haims has publicly stated, "Racism is agnostic to class, to the degrees you have, and to who your daddy is." Yet some readers have told Lythcott-Haims, "It can't have been *that* bad if you became student council president in high school." How does this repudiation of Lythcott-Haims's point of view and experience speak to the ways that Black people are not believed? What does this common response tell us about the allegation that we are color-blind or post-racial?

11. How do Lythcott-Haims's experiences compare to your experiences with racism and/or anti-Blackness? How do the painful moments in her memoir inform and complicate your understandings of race and of class in America?

The Writing and Its Readers

12. How is the term "Real American" used in public discourse today? Why do you think Lythcott-Haims chose this as the title of her memoir? What does the term mean to you?

13. Who are the intended audiences for this book? How do you know? Do you feel included in the audience for this book or do you feel like you are outside the intended audience? Why?

14. This book is in a nonstandard format (margins, font, chapters, page layout). Why do you think Lythcott-Haims made these choices? How does the format contribute to the message of the book?

Discussion Questions

15. Sometimes Lythcott-Haims switches from the first person to the second person "you." Why does she do this? Where do you recognize yourself as the "you" to whom she speaks? Did any of the references to "you" make you feel uncomfortable? If so, why?

16. Writers of memoir depict real-life events featuring real people. If you went back through the book, whose perspective would you be interested in knowing more about, and why? Did you feel any characters in the book were treated unfairly, and if so, why?

Being in Action

17. Toward the end of the book, Lythcott-Haims cites the story of a white male police officer who develops empathy for the Black children on his beat only once his Black wife gives birth to their son. Does this example make you feel optimistic or pessimistic about the likelihood that white people can learn to see Black people as fully human? Examining your feelings and assumptions, do you think you see Black people as fully human? Why or why not? If not, what would it take for you to do so?

St. Martin's
Griffin

18. Some readers say Lythcott-Haims has told truths few others are willing to say out loud. What do you think some of those truths are? Have you experienced any of (or anything like them) them in your own life? What are the benefits and consequences of sharing such truths?

19. What does it mean to be an "ally"? Who are the allies in this book? Who needs allies in our society? How can you use this book as a reference point for how to be a better ally?

20. Lythcott-Haims states that racism is antithetical to America's stated ideals of "liberty and justice for all." What allowed the framers of the Constitution and the authors of the Declaration of Independence to write about equality while condoning slavery and the inhumane treatment of Black people? How is that mind-set apparent through the present day? What do you think we can do about it?

For an online copy of these discussion questions, plus a list of further recommended reading from Julie Lythcott-Haims, go to https://us.macmillan.com/books/9781250137746.